Cambridge Opera Handbooks

Richard Wagner
Die Meistersinger von Nürnberg

Published titles

Richard Wagner
Die Meistersinger von Nürnberg

JOHN WARRACK

CAMBRIDGE
UNIVERSITY PRESS

Published by the Press Syndicate of the University of Cambridge
The Pitt Building, Trumpington Street, Cambridge CB2 1RP
40 West 20th Street, New York, NY 10011–4211, USA
10 Stamford Road, Oakleigh, Melbourne 3166, Australia

First published 1994

A catalogue record for this book is available from the British Library

Library of Congress cataloguing in publication data

Warrack, John Hamilton. 1928–
Richard Wagner, Die Meistersinger von Nürnberg / John Warrack.
    p.   cm. – (Cambridge opera handbooks)
Includes bibliographical references and index.
ISBN 0 521 44444 6 (hardback). – ISBN 0 521 44895 6 (paperback)
1. Wagner, Richard, 1813–1883. Meistersinger von Nürnberg.
I. Title. II. Title: Meistersinger von Nürnberg. III. Series.
ML410.WIA286   1994
782. 1 – dc20   93–39615   CIP   MN

ISBN 0 521 44444 6 hardback
ISBN 0 521 44895 6 paperback

Transferred to digital printing 2003

SN

Contents

Plates

General preface

This is a series of studies of individual operas, written for the serious opera-goer or record-collector as well as the student or scholar. Each volume has three main concerns. The first is historical: to describe the genesis of the work, its sources or its relation to literary prototypes, the collaboration between librettist and composer, and the first performance and subsequent stage history. The history is itself a record of changing attitudes towards the work, and an index of general changes of taste. The second is analytical and it is grounded in a very full synopsis which considers the opera as a structure of musical and dramatic effects. In most volumes there is also a musical analysis of a section of the score, showing how the music serves or makes the drama. The analysis, like the history, naturally raises questions of interpretation, and the third concern of each volume is to show how critical writing about an opera, like production and performance, can direct or distort appreciation of its structural elements. Some conflict of interpretation is an inevitable part of this account; editors of the handbooks reflect this – by citing classic statements, by commissioning new essays, by taking up their own critical position. A final section gives a select bibliography and guides to other sources.

Acknowledgments

I should like to thank Margaret Bent, Michael Curschmann, Denys Dyer, Kenneth Hamilton, Margaret Jacobs and Desmond Shawe-Taylor for reading parts of the text and giving me the benefit of their expert opinion, and in particular my wife for contribution, criticism, and constant support. I am also very grateful to the Librarians and Staff of the Taylorian Institute, the Bodleian Library and the Library of the Faculty of Music, Oxford, for their hospitality and help. At the Cambridge University Press, I gratefully acknowledge the editorial and copy-editing skills of Victoria Cooper and Janet Banks.

Abbreviations

ML   R. Wagner, *Mein Leben* (Munich, 1911; ed. M. Gregor-Dellin, 1963; trans. A. Gray, 1983)

SS   R. Wagner, *Sämtliche Schriften und Dichtungen* (ed. H. von Wolzogen and R. Sternfeld, Leipzig, 6th edn, 1914)

WWV   J. Deathridge, M. Geck and E. Voss, *Wagner Werk-Verzeichnis* (Mainz, 1986)

Composition and performance details

The various drafts and copies of the text of *Die Meistersinger* are referred to by the nomenclature established by J. Deathridge, M. Geck and E. Voss (eds.), *Wagner Werk-Verzeichnis* (*WWV*) (Mainz, 1986), as follows (not every printing is listed).

Text I The prose draft of 1845. Reprinted *Die Musik*, 20/1 (1902), pp. 1799–809, including sketch, with commentary by R. Sternfeld; *Sämtliche Schriften und Dichtungen* (*SS*), XI (1911), 344–55; trans. in R. Rayner, *Wagner and 'Die Meistersinger'* (Oxford, 1940), 16–24; M. Soden, *Richard Wagner: 'Die Meistersinger von Nürnberg'* (Frankfurt, 1983), pp. 144–57; trans. J. Ennis in *Wagner*, 8/1 (January 1987), pp. 13–22.

Text II The prose draft of 1861. Reprinted in Soden, *Richard Wagner*, pp. 159–87; *SS*, XI, pp. 356–78; trans. J. Ennis in *Wagner*, 9/3 (July 1988), pp. 106–15.

Text III Fair copy (1861), with some revisions, of Text II. Reprinted in *SS*, XI, p. 379–94.

Text IV First draft of libretto (25 January 1862). Facsimile in anon. [Bureau de dramaturgie de l'opéra national] (ed.), *Richard Wagner: 'Die Meistersinger von Nürnberg'* (Brussels, 1985).

Text V Fair copy of libretto (31 January 1862). Facsimile in E. Voss, *Richard Wagner: 'Die Meistersinger von Nürnberg'* (Mainz, 1983).

Text VI Second copy of libretto. Lost.

Text VII MS of five pages of drafts and alterations, principally concerning the Prize Song.

Music composed April 1862–September 1864 (with interruptions); January–March 1866; May 1866–24 October 1877.

First performance, Munich, Königliches Hof- und National-Theater, 21 June 1868, with Franz Betz (Hans Sachs), Kaspar Bausewein (Pogner), Karl Samuel Heinrich (Vogelgesang), Eduard

Sigl (Nachtigall), Gustav Hölzel (Beckmesser), Wilhelm Fisher (Kothner), Weixlstorfer (Zorn), Eduard Hoppe (Eisslinger), Pöppl (Moser), Franz Thoms (Ortel), Grasser (Hans Schwarz), Hayn (Hans Foltz), Franz Nachbaur (Walther), Max Schlosser (David), Mathilde Mallinger (Eva), Sophie Diez (Magdalene), Ferdinand Lang (Nightwatchman); sets Heinrich Döll, Christian Jank, Angelo Quaglio; conductor Hans von Bülow; producer Reinhard Hallwachs under the general direction of Wagner.

1   *The sources and genesis of the text*

Wagner has described in *Mein Leben* how the first idea for *Die Meistersinger von Nürnberg* came to him. Taking the cure at Marienbad in 1845, he tried to obey doctors' orders by abandoning all attempts at creative work and giving himself up to reading. The books he tells us he had with him were editions of Wolfram von Eschenbach and of the *Lohengrin* epic; and he describes how, so as to distract his mind from a full-scale re-engagement with his dormant *Lohengrin* ideas, he thought of writing a light opera.

From a few remarks in Gervinus' *History of German Literature*, I had formed a particularly vivid picture of Hans Sachs and the mastersingers of Nuremberg. I was especially intrigued by the institution of the marker and his function in rating master-songs. Without as yet knowing anything more about Hans Sachs and his poetic contemporaries, I conceived during a walk a comic scene in which the popular artisan-poet, by hammering upon his cobbler's last, gives the marker, who is obliged by circumstances to sing in his presence, his come-uppance for previous pedantic misdeeds during official singing contests, by inflicting upon him a lesson of his own. To me the force of the whole scene was concentrated in two points: on the one hand the marker with his slate covered with chalk marks and on the other Sachs with the shoes aloft, completed as a result of his hammering the marks in, whereby both indicate that the singing has been a failure. To this picture I now added a narrow, twisting Nuremberg alley, with neighbours, uproar and a street-fight – and suddenly my whole mastersingers comedy stood before me so vividly that, on the grounds that it was an especially merry subject, I felt justified in putting it on paper despite the doctor's instructions.[1]

As always with Wagner, in tracing the evolution of his ideas it is necessary to read between the lines, and not always to take the lines themselves at face value. But there seems no reason to doubt the truth of the incident described earlier in *Mein Leben* (though perhaps with advantages), when his part in the mockery of a certain Lauermann in Nuremberg led to a riot. Lauermann was a carpenter with singing ambitions, and, though suspicious of this tenor-voiced youth, was persuaded that Wagner was the great and influential bass Luigi Lablache. The tale includes an account of repeated mockery and humiliation of Lauermann, which even the half-drunk Wagner seems to have found too much to stomach, though the atmosphere of it survives into the treatment of Beckmesser. But the outcome was a moment of magic that haunted Wagner's imagination and returned to him to make the unforgettable end to Act II of the opera.

Out of this situation evolved an uproar, which through the shouting and clamour and an inexplicable growth in the number of participants in the struggle soon assumed a truly demoniacal character. It looked to me as if the whole town would break out into a riot, and I really thought myself to be once again involuntarily witnessing a revolution of which no-one had the slightest idea what it was all about. Then suddenly I heard a heavy thump, and as if by magic the whole crowd dispersed in every direction . . . One of the regular patrons . . . had felled one of the noisiest rioters . . . and it was the effect of this which scattered everybody so suddenly. Scarcely a minute after the fiercest tumult had been raging among hundreds of people, I was able to stroll arm-in-arm with my brother-in-law through the lonely moonlit streets, laughing and joking.[2]

The other incident he describes, that of the rival 'markers', seems to have come, as he says, entirely from his imagination.

But it was more than 'a few remarks' of Gervinus which contributed to the detail and atmosphere of the first prose sketch (Text I), which Wagner wrote in Marienbad. Georg Gottfried Gervinus's *Geschichte der poetischen National-Literatur der Deutschen* (Leipzig, 1850–4) (a book which, in this edition, Wagner had in his Dresden library) includes, as well as material on the epic subjects that were absorbing him, two long chapters on Mastersong and on Hans Sachs. That on Sachs deals chiefly with his work, especially his religious attitudes, and his relations with Luther's energetic and influential supporter Ulrich von Hutten and with Luther himself. In his *Handbuch der Geschichte der poetischen National-Literatur der Deutschen* (Leipzig, 3rd edn, 1844), another book which Wagner owned, Gervinus also makes a substantial contrast between Sachs and Hutten, the 'schlichte Bürgersmann gegen den gebildeten Rittersmann' ('the simple burgher contrasted with the cultured aristocrat'); and he sets out at some length Sachs's Lutheran stance. Text I retains a reference to them when Sachs advises the young man who has failed in his attempt at a

Mastersong to go back and study 'Hutten and the Wittemberger'; and there is also a mention of Sachs's most famous poem on Luther, *Die Wittembergisch Nachtigall*, the opening lines of which, hailing the Reformation, were to make the great salutation to Sachs himself in the final text of the *Festwiese* scene. Among Sachs's personal characteristics, we learn from Gervinus chiefly of an increasing irony in his writing as he grew older, coupled with a certain melancholy. He is referred to in the section on Mastersong as 'sitting grey and white like a dove, with a full beard, reading in a beautiful gold-bound book', not answering those who come to greet him but acknowledging their presence with an inclination of the head (this is closely matched in the stage directions for the opening of Act III of the opera). Text I takes up the irony as Sachs's prime characteristic rather than his nature as a dreamer (well-attested in accounts of him), which is also mentioned: only later was Wagner to understand the significance of dreams and dreaming to the work. Gervinus also describes how travelling singers found the courts no longer holding them in respect or giving them board and lodging; and how a healthy new rivalry arose, with artistic exchanges and contests and with prizes offered not by a society or school but by an individual. He declares the highest art to be the invention of a new *Ton*: the same text could be used to a different *Ton*, which must not come closer to that of another Master by more than four syllables. If successful, it would be recognised and the 'father' would baptise it with a name in the presence of 'godfathers'. There are other suggestions, such as the names of some Masters – Hans Folz and Kunz Zorn – and the devotion of the apprentices to their masters, which were to bear fruit at different stages of the growth of the text of the opera.[3]

The First Draft (Text I) is dated 'Marienbad, 6 July 1845', and includes a rough drawing of the layout of Act II, with a curving street separating the houses of Sachs and the Guildmaster. It runs to something over four thousand words, in the old German *Schrift* which Wagner used until 1848.

In Act I, a young man approaches a young girl from a wealthy bourgeois family (neither is named) in St Sebaldus's Church. The son of an impoverished knight, he has come to Nuremberg to seek membership of the Mastersingers, and the two have promptly fallen in love. The Marker also wants to marry the girl, whose father has decreed that she shall only be given to the Master who wins a public singing contest decided by the people. The housekeeper Magdalene calls the girl away, though not before she has made her own amorous exchanges with the apprentice

4 Die Meistersinger von Nürnberg

David. The Masters assemble as the apprentices prepare the chapel. They do not really trust Sachs, and wonder whether he means well by the Guild. The Marker hopes to win the girl, and the Guildmaster wishes him well, insisting, in the face of the Marker's fears about the people's judgement, that the girl must have a say. Sachs arrives, and the roll is called. The Guildmaster announces his plan for the people to have first vote for once, so as to increase the popular standing of the art, then the Masters, and his daughter the casting vote if they disagree. The young man sings, believing that he is before a group of Minnesingers. Sachs reads out the rules with some irony, to the Masters' disquiet; he also upsets the young man with his sharpness. The young man surprises them by offering Siegfried and Grimmhilde as his subject, then (to further shock) Parzifal, in Wolfram's *Ton*. His song in praise of poetry is too heavily marked before he has even finished. Sachs is sympathetic, and, laughing at the Mastersingers, challenges the Marker to do better. The Marker refuses, claiming that Sachs would not do well, either, were he not held in high esteem, and complaining about the non-delivery of a new pair of shoes for the competition. The meeting breaks up in confusion, with the young man defeated.

In Act II, it is evening and Magdalene returns to her house, passing David on her way. The Guildmaster commends the Marker to his daughter, who is upset to hear of the young man's failure. Magdalene tells her that the Marker wants her to remain at her window so that he may woo her with his trial song as a serenade. Sachs sends David to bed and settles down; he recalls the young man, and falls into a tender, visionary mood. The young man enters, planning to elope with the girl; Sachs, overhearing, feels he must prevent this. The girl asks Magdalene to take her place at the window and to indicate her dislike of the song. The girl returns in Magdalene's clothes, but she and the young man recognise Sachs in the light of his shop: she warns that her father has often told her Sachs is not to be trusted. They are about to go when they hear the nightwatchman's horn, and are obliged to hide. The Marker appears and Sachs, having overheard everything, takes up his place at his last and, when the Marker begins to sing, joins in with a ribald song. He explains to the angry Marker that he must finish his shoes. The Marker agrees to let Sachs mark his song with blows on the last; they are thereby finished, while the Marker manages also to finish his song (to disapproving headshakes from the figure in the window). David misunderstands the situation, and his attack on the Marker precipitates 'general disarray, questions and raging'. Sachs pushes the girl back into her house and pulls the young man into his shop. All is suddenly quiet; the nightwatchman returns to an empty street.

In Act III, Sachs is discovered neglecting his work and surrounded by his books. He reflects on the decline of poetry and wonders if he, a cobbler, is the only man to comprehend the great heritage of German art. Magdalene calls from outside for David, who is told to get on with his work. He interrupts Sachs's musings by singing his cobbler's song; Sachs is at first annoyed, but later joins in. The young man appears, and is reproached by Sachs for trying to elope with the girl; there must be a fair contest for her. He confesses his disappointment with the Masters, and tells Sachs that he has written heroic lays and also a love song (played in the orchestra). This interests Sachs, and draws him into further reflections on the decline of poetry, as a weapon against foolishness and superstition, in favour of reason and philosophy, which in turn will have to be defended. Only in the distant future may Sachs himself and earlier Masters be rediscovered: meanwhile, the young man should return to his castle and study Hutten and Luther. The girl returns, and in a trio she reproaches Sachs, who is defended by the young man; they all leave. Two alternative versions of the text are now given. In the original, the Marker appears and pockets the song he finds on the table, admitting his theft on the return of Sachs, who makes him a present of it but warns him to find the right tune for it. In Wagner's second thoughts, written in the margin, the Marker is first angry with Sachs over the previous night's events, and the ruination of his song; Sachs offers him the young man's song, which he says he himself wrote in his younger days, promising not to admit to it and then giving him some malicious advice on how to sing it. In St John's meadow, small festival processions approach from the city. There are games and dances. The Masters enter, and Sachs is acclaimed. The Guildmaster pleases the people with his explanation of what is to take place. The unpopular Marker appears and makes a mess of singing the song, to general amusement; the girl refuses him. He furiously exposes the song as by Sachs, who insists that it only needs good singing to the right melody. He will not sing it himself, as he is too old to be wooing. The young man now steps forward: the people overrule the Masters' objections, and his triumph makes them realise that they must give him the prize. But when he refuses membership of the Guild, Sachs, half-ironically, half in earnest, defends the good things in the Masters' work. All join in praising Sachs, and the bridal procession leads the others back into the city. Added to the MS at a later date is the couplet:

Zerging' das heil'ge römische Reich in Dunst,
uns bliebe doch die heil'ge deutsche Kunst.
(Were the Holy Roman Empire to dissolve into mist,
we should still have holy German art.)[4]

In studying this sketch, and doing so from the vantage point of knowledge of the final work, it is important to remember that it was intended for a light opera (whatever Wagner may have meant by that). We have his own testimony for this, and the MS, on a greenish quarto paper, is headed 'Kom. Oper in 3 Acten'. The document bears signs of the haste with which it was written. The narrative is breathless, expressed partly in note form, partly in complete sentences, and from time to time contains snatches of dialogue, as if phrases for musical setting were appearing in Wagner's mind as he jotted down the plot outline. There are several additions – the final couplet, the extra passage concerning the mechanics of Beckmesser acquiring the Prize Song, and a note under the change of scene in Act III making reconciliation between David and Magdalene. There are also some grammatical errors, such as 'der Merker habe ihr begegnet', and, in the footnote providing for Magdalene and the girl to change their clothing, the word 'Begleitung' for 'Bekleidung' (perhaps Wagner's Saxon accent got the better of him).

As it stands, the sketch outlines an opera that pokes fun at the pedantic Masters and allows true love to win through. However, it already implies a good deal more than that. In 1845, Wagner had endured rejection by one operatic establishment in Paris and frustration at the hands of another through the sloppy standards prevailing in Dresden. His irritation was, moreover, increasingly coloured both by his own reforming zeal and by political affiliations that were to lend a revolutionary enthusiasm to his ideas. Even in the sketch, there is a polemic element that carries implications beyond light satire. The only three characters of any substance are Sachs, the Marker and the young man. The latter is also sometimes referred to in Act II as 'the lover' (and the girl as 'the beloved'): he is uncertainly balanced between ardent suitor and impassioned reformer, arriving in Nuremberg filled with *Minnesinger* ideals and notions which make him seem at once more innocently old-fashioned and more creatively exuberant than the Mastersingers. He has, he tells Sachs, written heroic verses praising the Emperors, but also love songs. Standing before the Masters in his first trial, he attempts to sing of Siegfried and Grimmhilde or of Parzifal, and clearly sees himself in the mould of the master he acknowledges in the work's eventual version, Walther von der Vogelweide (who also makes an appearance in the opera Wagner had just finished, *Tannhäuser*). In his person, art and love are in fruitful contact, and this contact is emphasised by the crabbed and warped nature of their relationship in the person of the Marker. However, art and love have not yet found the subtly balanced associations that lie at the heart of the opera.

The character of Sachs is at this stage highly equivocal. Ernest Newman finds that, 'In his first form Wagner's Sachs was a rather cynical, ironic, embittered character, who, apart from his advocacy of the cause of the young Knight, reminds us comparatively little of the wise, kindly, mellow poet-philosopher he ultimately becomes in Wagner's treatment of him'[5] (that this description says too little about the darker side of Sachs's nature is not at present relevant). Robert M. Raynor describes him as, at this point, 'an unpleasantly ironical character who is more or less disliked by all who know him'.[6] Richard Turner argues that these are misconceptions. Pointing out that the brevity of the sketch could not but make the characters seem more abrupt, he suggests that Sachs's unpopularity with the Mastersingers should indicate not his meanness of spirit but theirs, that the irony with which he reads the *Tabulatur* is directed not against the young knight but against its confining rules, and that his misgivings spring from his concern about the future of poetry. Turner also argues that when the girl beseeches the lover not to trust Sachs, for she has often been told how deceitful he is, it is the voice of her father, the head of the Guild, which she is echoing.[7] Sachs later defends the Mastersingers against the young man's rejection of them in a tone 'half-ironic, half-serious', as befits a man with a regard for tradition but one who finds that tradition atrophying.

The truth is that Sachs, the subtlest and most complicated character of the three, is at this primitive stage naturally also the least consistent and complete. Moreover, Wagner had yet to read Schopenhauer. Yet he has instinctively set down a number of details whose implications he may not yet have understood but which were there for his later crafting once Schopenhauer had given a centre to his ideas. One of the few passages in which he writes some quite extended dialogue is in the scene in Act III where he makes Sachs argue wryly about the coming decline of poetry: there is already here an old man's more considered engagement with the role of art in human lives than is evinced by the poetic *Schwärmerei* of the young man and his impetuous delight in the *Minnesinger*. Yet Sachs is constantly detached and ironic, lacking the depth of human perspective necessary for the subtle connections Wagner was to make between life (and love) and art. An obvious reason is that the Mastersingers were as yet faceless adversaries, lacking the individual humanity that was to give them a more sympathetic quality, in their ordinary human fallibility, and with it a connection to Sachs himself. They are still propaganda, not art. But Sachs himself is uncertainly set forth. There can as yet be no sense of his integration in the society whose nature and traditions he is to uphold, nor of his friendship with the still uncharacterised Pogner, nor of the delicate feelings between him and Eva. His benevolence to the young man is not in question; but nor is a certain malevolence towards the Marker, and though Wagner was never wholly to expunge this from Sachs's nature, it was to be absorbed into a character whose largeness of humanity can embrace it. Already Wagner was aware of the problem, since he tried out two ways of transferring the Prize Song into the Marker's possession. Neither is satisfactory, but nor is the final version; for if one can perhaps account for Sachs's discomfiture of Beckmesser in the serenade scene as his half-latent rivalry for Eva emerging in the form of rough Teutonic humour (recalling Wagner's own part in the mockery of the incompetent singer Lauermann), there is still the uncomfortable matter of Sachs permitting Beckmesser to humiliate himself in the *Festwiese*. Aware of this problem, some producers have tried having Sachs recall Beckmesser after Walther's triumph so as to take part in the reconciliation and rejoicing. Yet seeds of richer fruit have already been sown. In Act II, near the start, Sachs leans out of his shop, reluctant to go indoors, and 'thinks of the young man and falls into a gentle, tender reverie'. There is no way of knowing whether or not Wagner already had an aria in mind here, though the mention of a reverie makes it seem likely: it is, of course, the first glimpse of the *Flieder* monologue. Again, Sachs's melancholy reflections with his great book at the start of Act III are as yet only over the decline of poetry, on which he 'continues to philosophise'. There is the occasion, though not yet the content, of the *Wahn* monologue.

One of the few people to see this sketch was Mathilde Wesendonk, to whom Wagner gave it as a present. He appears then to have forgotten it, or at any rate to have let it recede to the back of his mind; for his next reference to it comes in *Eine Mitteilung an meine Freunde* of 1851. Here he describes how he had decided to write a comic opera, partly so as to win a success on the German stage for his other achievements, and how his eye had fallen on a piece whose song contest would make a light-hearted counterpart to that of *Tannhäuser*.

Just as with the Athenians a comic satyr play would follow a tragedy, so there suddenly came to me the image of a comic piece that could be attached to my *Singers' Contest on the Wartburg* as a richly allusive satyr play . . . This was *The Mastersingers of Nuremberg*, headed by Hans Sachs. I conceived of Hans Sachs as the last manifestation of the artistically productive folk spirit, and set against him in this quality the petit bourgeois Masters, for whose absurd, poetry-by-Tabulatur pedantry I found embodiment in the Marker. This Marker, as is well known (or, to our critics, perhaps not), was the appointed observer of the singers' guild, who had to 'mark' with strokes the performer's mistakes contravening the rules: someone who had scored a certain number of strokes was 'sung out'. The oldest member of the Guild now offers the hand of his young daughter to whichever member of the Guild wins the prize in a public singing contest that is about to be held. The Marker, who is already the girl's suitor, finds he has a rival in the person of a young man of noble birth, who is inspired by reading the Heldenbuch and the old Minnesingers to leave his impoverished and crumbling ancestral castle so as to learn the art of Mastersong in Nuremberg. He applies to join the Guild, being further inspired by promptly falling in love with the girl who is to be the prize, 'since only a Master of the Guild can win'; put to the test, he sings an enthusiastic song in praise of women, but this arouses an unprecedented number of objections from the Marker so that the candidate is already 'sung out' with only half his song. Sachs, who likes the young man, then (in his interests) foils his desperate attempt to elope with the girl; Sachs thereby also finds occasion to enrage the Marker. Having previously abused Sachs over an unfinished pair of shoes with the aim of humiliating him, the Marker appears by night under the girl's window so as to try out the song with which he hopes to succeed, as a serenade, and thereby to ensure her deciding voice at the prize-giving. Sachs, whose workshop stands opposite the serenaded house, begins singing loudly when the Marker does because – as he explains to the infuriated man – this is necessary if he is going to stay awake so late over his work; no-one knows better than the Marker that this work is urgent since he himself has pressed so hard for his shoes. Eventually he persuades the wretched man to stop: he will only be allowed to continue if the mistakes which Sachs finds in the song according to *his* feelings can be marked in *his* manner – as a cobbler – with a blow on the shoe for each one. Now the Marker sings: Sachs smites repeatedly on the last. The Marker leaps up angrily; Sachs asks him calmly if he is done with the song. 'Not by any means', shouts the Marker. Sachs laughingly brings the shoes out of the shop and explains that they have just been finished by means of the 'marks'. The Marker bawls the rest of his song uninterruptedly in confusion, beneath the vigorously shaking head of the female form at the window. Disconsolately, he asks Sachs next day for a new song for the bridal contest; Sachs gives him a poem by the young knight without telling him how he acquired it: he only warns him to take care to find a suitable 'Weise' to sing to it. The vain Marker has every confidence in himself, and sings it, before the assembled Masters and people, to a completely unsuitable and distorting melody so that once more he fails, this time decisively. He furiously accuses Sachs of having tricked him with a bad poem; Sachs explains that the poem is good but needs to be sung to an appropriate 'Weise'. It is agreed that whoever knows the right 'Weise' shall be the winner. The young knight succeeds in this, and wins his bride; however, he rejects the offer of admission to the Guild. So Sachs makes a humorous defence of the art of Mastersong, closing with the couplet:

Were the Holy Roman Empire to dissolve into mist,
We should still have holy German art.[8]

There are several changes in detail here, but also a crucial shift in emphasis, showing that Wagner's ideas had matured and perhaps also that the subject had never been dislodged from some corner of his mind. In placing greater importance on Sachs as a creative figure, Wagner moves the young man into a somewhat different position in the drama: he now sings, for instance, not of heroic poetry but in praise of women. He is at this stage less the challenger to tradition, ironically observed by Sachs: indeed, there is no longer any mention of irony in connection with Sachs, whose final defence of the Mastersingers is now 'humorous' (*mit Humor*), nor the strong sense of antagonism between him and the Guild. Of course the paragraph in *Eine Mitteilung* is a description of an earlier scheme, not a draft or synopsis; but it indicates that Sachs had moved more decisively to the centre of Wagner's attention, and Wagner himself confirms that he no longer felt irony to be the suitable means for expressing his humorous intentions.

By Wagner's account in *Mein Leben*, his next engagement with *Die Meistersinger* came in a revelatory flash in Venice. Depressed after the notorious *Tannhäuser* fiasco in Paris in March 1861, he spent much of the remainder of the year travelling; and he was glad to accept an invitation from the Wesendonks to meet them that November in Venice, where they were to have a short holiday, and spent the 7th to the 13th with them. He was perplexed to find them more interested in the art of Venice than in the details of his plight, happy though they were to cheer him up by sharing their pleasures with him. 'I have to admit that despite all my apathy Titian's *Assumption of the Virgin* in the great hall of the Doges made a most exalting impression on me, so that by this inspiration I found my old creative powers awakening within me with almost their original primordial power. I decided to write *Die Meistersinger*.'[9] Apart from wrongly locating the Titian in the Doge's Palace, Wagner was indulging in one of his feats of constructive memory.[10] He liked the idea of the inspirational moment as the starting point for a work of art, as with the radiant Good Friday morning he pretended had set *Parsifal* working in his mind, and also perhaps with the so-called La Spezia vision and *The Ring*; and his good-humoured acceptance of factual correction on some of these matters did not destroy for him their artistic truth. Later, he was to deny the impact of Venetian works of art on him to Mathilde (letter of 21 December 1861);[11] however, the inspiration he drew from the Titian was recalled in Schopenhauerian vein many years later, when on his last visit to Venice he stood again before it and (according to Cosima, a great Titian-lover), 'the glowing head of the Virgin Mary recalls to him his idea of the sexual urge: this unique and mighty force, now freed of all desire, the Will enraptured and redeemed'.[12] This comment perhaps gives the clue to the otherwise inexplicable source of his inspiration in Titian: his awareness in Venice that his relationship with Mathilde must be transfigured by renunciation finds an outcome in the renunciation of Eva by Sachs, when he even quotes *Tristan*, though of course this vital element in the opera was not to emerge until later.

In fact, a resumption of work on *Die Meistersinger* was already in his mind. His travels that August had taken him through Nuremberg, where the second Pan-German Choral Festival (Deutsches Sängerfest) had been held on 21–24 July. Here, 240 choral groups comprising some 5,500 participants sang, as the climax, a paean of hope for a united Germany to an audience of 14,000 in a specially built hall outside the Laufertor. It is inconceivable that Wagner should not have heard of this and remembered his old idea; indeed, his *Festwiese* scene is far closer in many details to the various nineteenth-century Nuremberg celebrations of which the Festival was but one manifestation than to their sixteenth-century counterpart (a kinship acknowledged when the 1912 festival included a performance of the closing scene of *Die Meistersinger*). Moreover, his impoverished state that autumn had led him to ponder ways of improving his finances during the delays that were afflicting the Vienna production of *Tristan*. Having sounded out his publisher Franz Schott about a loan on 17 October, he wrote again on the 30th with a plan for *Die Meistersinger*. It would be, he told Schott, a light, popular piece making no demands either upon production or upon such expensive items as star tenors and 'great tragic sopranos', and for the role of Hans Sachs requiring no more than any competent bass or baritone. Small German theatres would find the work within their resources, while the larger ones would be able to revel in the big choruses. Wagner even maps out a schedule: the text would be ready by January 1862, the first act of the full score by the end of March, the second act by the end of July, and the third by the end of September; while the first performance could take place in Munich in November.

It is impossible to know how disingenuous Wagner was being. He did manage to finish the second prose draft (Text II) and to send its revised version (Text III) to Schott in January; but he must have had more than an inkling that the work was showing signs of outstripping his account of it. Leaving Venice abruptly, he turned his mind to the music of *Die Meistersinger*, the poem of which (he assures us in *Mein Leben*), 'I had retained in my mind only in its earliest form'.[13] This is to overlook the progress the subject had made in his mind from 1845 to the time of the account in *Eine Mitteilung* of 1851; against that must be set his remark, in *Mein Leben*, that he had 'conceived the main part of the overture in C major with the greatest clarity'[14] (he also described this in a letter to Mathilde on 21 December 1861).[15] The word he used for 'main part' is *Hauptteil*, which could be taken in different ways. In any case, two points of interest arise. The absence of any reference to Sachs in the overture suggests that Wagner was indeed remembering his original treatment, though even so it is surprising to find so central a character omitted. Further, the melodic material associated with the Mastersingers in the overture is derived from an example in Wagenseil's history of Nuremberg and the Mastersingers, which Wagner did not then know. Newman suggests that, given his earlier interest in the subject, he might easily have come across the melody in some other book and remembered it; a more likely hypothesis is that Wagner was preferring the imaginative idea of an irresistible creative impulse overcoming him, as his train climbed through the majestic Dolomites, to more mundane facts. Some mixture of the two is perhaps even more likely, namely that Wagner did indeed ponder the nature of the overture on the journey, finding elements in the Wagenseil melody providing suitable material once he had pored over the book when he reached Vienna.

Wagner drafted the second sketch (Text II) early in November 1861, making a slightly altered copy (Text III) for Schott which he completed on the 18th. The work has now become (Text II) a 'Grosse komische Oper in 3 Aufzügen', with the following characters:

> Hans Sachs, cobbler (bass)
> Bogler, elder of the Guild (bass)
> Hanslich, Town Clerk, Marker to the Guild (bass)
> Konrad von Stolzing (tenor)
> Emma, Bogler's daughter (soprano)
> Kathrine, her nurse (mezzo-soprano)
> David, Sachs's apprentice (tenor)
> Mastersingers, burgers and women from all the Guilds.
> The people.

> Nuremberg, about the middle of the sixteenth century.

The new plot may be summarised as follows.

Act I. Scene 1 Before the sacristy of St Sebaldus's Church, a chorale is
ending a service attended by Emma and Kathrine. Konrad von Stolzing
leans against a pillar, exchanging amorous signs with Emma. She is
restrained by Kathrine, who nevertheless agrees to contrive a meeting.
Konrad has been welcomed in her father's house the day before, having
left his crumbling estate, and they have fallen in love. He learns that she
is to be betrothed to the man who wins the coming Singers' Contest, and
resolves to seek immediate admittance to the Mastersingers' Guild. David
makes his own amorous exchanges with Kathrine, and the apprentices
prepare for the trial. **Scene 2** Konrad is instructed by David in the names
and positions of the Mastersingers, and in their rules; he goes into some
detail about the mistakes and the role of the Marker. This is to be the
knowledgeable and arrogant Hanslich, who is not on good terms with
Sachs but hopes to win Emma. **Scene 3** The Mastersingers enter, headed
by Hanslich and Bogler, who insists that Emma must have the final say in
choice of husband. Konrad delights Bogler by seeking entrance to the
Guild, and Bogler then announces his intention of trying to recover the
honour of the Guild with the coming contest (the outline of his address is
as in the opera). Sachs suggests that, while art must follow rules, it is
good for those who do not know the rules to have a chance of judging:
the contest is for the uninstructed, with the girl's vote recognised. He is
overruled, and has to content himself with the thought that at least the
girl has a vote. Konrad explains that he wishes to become a Nuremberger
and, since he has loved poetry from childhood, also a Mastersinger. There
are doubts about him being eligible, as he is not already a member of any
Guild, but (with Sachs for and Hanslich against) he is accepted for trial
on Bogler's casting vote. Various melodies are offered him, and he
chooses the most euphonious-sounding. The rules are explained to him.
Discouraged, he begins in the style of the *Minnesinger*. The Marker shakes
his head, and makes David mark the mistakes. Eventually Konrad turns
away in despair, singing only for the girl he loves; the furious Marker
interrupts him, telling him that the slate is full before he has even finished.
Konrad appeals to the Masters, and an argument follows. Only Sachs
defends him as having sung well despite the mistakes; Hanslich offers to
substantiate these, and when Sachs queries his competence in this case,
berates Sachs and adds that he still hasn't had his bridegroom's shoes
delivered. Sachs agrees that Hanslich needs a good *Spruch* (axiom or
aphorism), and might write one on his shoes. The meeting breaks up.

Act II Outside his shop, Sachs is reflecting on Konrad's song; it seemed so
old yet was so new, so strange yet so familiar, so irregular yet so logical,
like a bird in spring, inimitable yet well known, inspired by necessity, a
bird with a sweet voice that may have alarmed the Masters but pleases
Hans Sachs. Kathrine and Emma enter and speak in low voices: Emma
has heard of Konrad's failure, but Kathrine now brings a message from
Hanslich asking her to be at the window of her house to hear his doubtless prize-winning serenade so as to gain her vote. Ill at ease, she asks
Kathrine to change clothes with her; Kathrine agrees, hoping to stimulate

David's jealousy. Konrad appears, and they plan to elope. When they hear the Nightwatchman's horn, she disappears to change her clothes. Sachs has overheard, and resolves to prevent them: when they reappear together, he throws a beam of light upon them. Konrad is unafraid, claiming Sachs as his only friend, but Emma says he can't be trusted and is very strict. Konrad is about to lead her away when they see Hanslich approaching; she restrains him, and they hide. Sachs, overhearing, busies himself ('Now I must write the *Spruch* well on the shoes'). When he breaks into song, Hanslich berates him despite Sachs's insistence that he is only finishing the shoes. Hanslich accuses him of malice and of inferiority as an artist and as Marker; Sachs suggests that he must practise, then, and must begin now by striking the shoes and perhaps making a good *Spruch*. Only when he starts up does Hanslich reluctantly give in and start his *Minnegesang* to the figure he sees in the window. The style is 'pedantic and ridiculous', and the combination of Sachs's hammer-blows and the disguised Kathrine's head-shaking rouses Hanslich to fury, his song still incomplete when the shoes are ready. David is aroused by the noise and, misunderstanding the situation, attacks Hanslich, disturbing the neighbours. Sachs intervenes to prevent the lovers escaping, pushing Emma back into her house, holding onto Konrad and despatching David to bed with his strap. The Nightwatchman's horn quickly disperses the mob, and when he arrives he finds himself in a deserted, moonlit alley.

Act III. Scene 1 Sachs is sitting in his sunny workshop next morning absorbed in a large folio. David slips in nervously, not daring to disturb his master and then confessing that he had attacked Hanslich, whose shoes he has meanwhile delivered, because of the serenade to his Magdalene [*sic*], whom he recognised, and because of the insults to Sachs himself. He is about to ask permission to marry Magdalene when Sachs snaps the book shut and the startled David vanishes. Alone, Sachs reflects on his searching the chronicles of world history for an explanation of the *Wahn* that can seize men (there follows the outline of the opera's *Wahn* monologue up to the mention of the glow-worm and the *Kobold*). Konrad enters, pale from lack of sleep and resentful of Sachs's interference. Sachs in turn reproves him but assures him that his own fondness for the girl makes him want to be sure of Konrad's good intentions. Konrad is annoyed, and reflects that the true poet is what the ordinary man becomes when in love; he could only calm himself by writing a poem last night. Sachs reads it, while the orchestra plays the melody. '*Wahn* again, lovely and tender, filled with passion, both wild and gentle – *allüberall Wahn*. What a wild Kobold achieved, let a nobler *Wahn* now accomplish. Let us shake people out of their rut for a while.' When they have gone to dress for the festival, Hanslich limps in, the orchestra portraying his sorry state 'like a pantomime'. He grabs the love song, concealing it when he hears Sachs returning. After complaining of the shoes, he asks for help with a new song, now that Sachs has ruined the effect of his own on Eva [*sic*]. When Sachs denies writing love songs, he produces Konrad's. Sachs tells him to use it if he likes; he will not claim authorship, but he warns Hanslich to learn it well and to find the right melody, about which Hanslich is confident. When he goes, Eva enters, complaining about her new shoes; Sachs can find no fault in them, and then, noticing her caught by Konrad's gaze, reflects on the trouble he has with his cobbling, which he would have given up long ago were he not also a poet. He encourages the lovers' hopes of success in the contest, and Eva tells him that were it not for Konrad she would have chosen him. In a brief intermezzo, David enters; Magdalene comes to take Eva off, Sachs tells David to shut up shop, and the three men leave.

During the change to **Scene 2**, the orchestra plays a festival march beginning quietly and increasing in volume. In St John's Meadow outside the city, decorated barges are bringing the people along the River Pegel to the festival. On one side is a raised platform with tiered benches; young men are marshalling the crowds and the arriving Guilds. Finally there enter the Mastersingers, led by Bogler with Eva at his side. Sachs introduces himself as *Festspruchsprecher* (Festival Spokesman) and explains the import of Bogler's gesture; let laymen in particular pay attention to the arts and learn from this festival. He is greeted with applause, and Hanslich is encouraged to feel he is under the protection of so popular a figure. Stepping forward, Hanslich tries to catch Eva's eye, and begins his song. Its ludicrous distortion of Konrad's poem astonishes the Mastersingers, embarrassed by the people's ridicule. Hanslich furiously accuses Sachs, who protests that he did not write the song, which only needs good singing. Konrad sings it so beautifully that the audience quietly joins in the final verse, then breaking into applause with which the Mastersingers are forced to sympathise. Konrad receives the garland and Bogler betrothes him to Eva. But when he is offered membership of the Mastersingers, he violently refuses. Sachs intervenes, and in a powerful song praises the Guild's achievements in encouraging the arts, in reconciling adversaries (even those who come to blows in the street by night), and, as representative of all the Guilds, in striving to put an end to folly with a nobler *Wahn*. So let everyone cultivate the good and beautiful. As Sachs is crowned by the girls, led by Eva, they sing of how even if the Holy Roman Empire should dissolve, still holy German art shall endure.

This summary of Wagner's text (which runs to some 5,500 words) can do no more than indicate the outline of the plot as it then stood, and isolate certain significant similarities to, and differences from, the final libretto. Though Wagner wrote Text II out again in fair copy for Schott (Text III), changing many of the forms of expression, he kept most of the material the same. The increasing emphasis on *Wahn* is discussed elsewhere in this volume (see Chapter 4): the actual plot differs only in small details and emphases. However, some of the names have changed. Bogler (now a goldsmith) and Hanslich acquire Christian names, Thomas and Veit respectively. Emma and Kathrine have already turned into Eva and Magdalene by Act III of Text II, as can be seen. At some point during his consideration of the outline, Wagner must have realised the resonances possible by associating Eva with Eve in paradise. Not until the drafting of the libretto (Text IV) did he discover another resonance and rechristen Konrad as Walther, after his artistic forebear, 'von der Vogelweide'. St Sebald's Church is now simply 'the church': possibly Wagner already had it in mind eventually to make the church St Catherine's when he changed Kathrine to Magdalene, but the renown of St Sebald's as containing the saint's shrine, the masterpiece of Sachs's contemporary Peter Vischer, did lose him a point of artistic reference in his celebration of Nuremberg and German art. There is one other major point of difference concerning Texts II and III: the former has, appended to it, a long set of notes about Mastersong drawn from Wagner's reading of Wagenseil. It begins with the listing of twelve Mastersingers by the names they eventually bear in the opera (with the minor rechristening, in the opera, of Fritz Zorn as Balthasar Zorn); Nikolaus Vogel (absent ill in the opera) is included and so now are Veit Pogner and Sixtus Beckmesser. There is then a set of notes on the *Tabulatur*, with the faults it categorises, a summary of the rules and the conditions of song-trials, and a list of the tones. These find their way into Text III, which further emphasises the seriousness of Sachs's feelings towards Eva as part of the steady deepening of his character. Apart from these differences, Texts II and III can be treated as similar in considering the advances made on Text I.

Several changes in plot and characterisation in Texts II/III may be singled out for mention. First, the young knight who left his decaying castle in Text I and *Eine Mitteilung* to learn the art of Mastersong (singing at his trial of art in the former, of women in the latter) has now come to Nuremberg to do business with Bogler, and at the trial embarks upon a given melody 'in the style of the old *Minnesinger*' before being carried away by his love for the girl as he sings. In Text I, the Guildmaster proposes that the contest shall be decided first by the people, then the Mastersingers, and then, if they cannot agree, by his daughter on a casting vote. Texts II and III have Bogler making the Mastersingers award the prize, with his daughter retaining the veto and final decision; this now carries with it the power to reject the prizewinner, though not to choose anyone else. It is Sachs who tries, unsuccessfully, to let the people decide, and this version, with the opposition to Sachs less acute, survives into the opera. The intention seems to be to advance Sachs as the champion of *vox populi*, and to make more palatable the notion of the heroine being treated as a trophy.

Wagner has also tried to resolve one of the awkwardnesses that occur from time to time in his plots. It is necessary for Eva and Magdalene to change clothes so as to disguise Eva for the escape and to create the necessary misunderstanding in David's mind. In Text I, the girl asks Magdalene (who agrees 'for her own reasons') to change. The young man is surprised, having (perhaps wisely) not been told of the Marker's intended serenade: he is silenced by her assurance that she regards these circumstances as Heaven's blessing on their flight. Wagner adds a marginal note making provision for a later explanatory narration. This is thoroughly unconvincing, and the problem is skirted round in *Eine Mitteilung*. In Texts II and III, Emma 'beseeches Kathrine to change clothes with her and to appear in her stead at the window. Kathrine agrees, hoping that David, who sleeps opposite, will have his jealousy aroused and so declare his love.' So far, so good. But Wagner needed, for reasons more important than plot mechanics, to include the scene in which the delicate amorous affection between Sachs and Eva is indicated, and this she could hardly conduct in Magdalene's clothes. He therefore had to invent the device whereby Magdalene tells Eva she has a secret message from Beckmesser and takes her into the house, leaving Sachs alone for his *Flieder* monologue. But Magdalene cannot now do the natural thing and tell Eva in private about Beckmesser's intended serenade, since the audience would remain in the dark about the reasons for the change of clothes; and so there has to be an extra scene in which the subject is taken up at greater length after Eva's scene with Sachs. It is a cumbersome addition, but it does have the effect of separating the two more intense scenes when Eva reveals first her agitated emotions towards Sachs and then her ecstatic ones towards Walther. The feelings between Sachs and Eva are barely indicated in Texts II and III: she does tell him, in the scene when she complains of her shoes, that if she didn't love the knight so much she'd choose Sachs, provided that he won the prize, but there is no suggestion that this is anything more than a rush of affectionate enthusiasm. Wagner, incidentally, is surely here making use of the legend whereby St Crispin, the patron saint of cobblers mentioned in the *Festwiese* scene, fell in love with the Emperor's daughter Ursula, who pretended that her shoes fitted badly so as to give him the opportunity of stroking her foot and declaring himself. Once Wagner had seen how this emotion would enrich the drama and strengthen his essential ideas within it, he needed to prepare for the erotic tensions and resolutions that were to fill the shoe-fitting scene.

It will also be noticed that in the growing richness and significance of the character of Sachs, he now praises the Mastersingers in the final scene no longer 'half ironically, half in earnest', but wholeheartedly; and that the Prize Song is no longer one of the young man's previous works but the fruit of his sleepless night after the riot. This is not yet the stuff of dreams, but, like other elements in the revised text, it indicates how by 1861 a much richer soil was fertilising Wagner's rapidly growing imaginative powers.

Even without knowledge of the opera's final text (let alone of the music that was no doubt already beginning to form in Wagner's mind), it is clear that there has been a significant change between the first draft and the next two. Text I, which shows Sachs in an unformed state but strikingly marked with cynicism, was intended for a comic opera, conceived in a satirical spirit that has a strong salting of malice in it. Wagner's resentment at what he saw as pedantic obstructions placed in his path by reactionary critics gives the text sharpness but not the matter of true comedy; and if it had survived as no more than one of the drafts for abandoned projects in his collected writings, posterity would doubtless have dismissed it with comments about his sure instinct in avoiding the light comic vein for which *Das Liebesverbot* had proved that he had little gift. But Wagner was, in this sense, his own posterity. By the time of *Eine Mitteilung*, when the subject had shifted a little in his mind, he was opposing the *Ironie* that had motivated his original idea with *Heiterkeit*: that is to say, no longer 'irony' tingeing his artistic views and aims, but 'cheerful humour' possessing an emotional force coming from deep in individual humanity. For the latter, his personal circumstances were still unfavourable. Texts II and III, taken without knowledge of anything else, would indicate a work rich in possibilities, though of course no-one could foresee how Wagner would realise them. Much that would not have gone into these notes was fermenting in his mind, and many ingredients that could not be identified from internal evidence were being poured into the mixture upon which the yeast of his genius was working.

One of Wagner's first acts on returning to Vienna had been to study Jakob Grimm's *Ueber den altdeutschen Meistergesang* (Göttingen, 1811); he had already been excited by Grimm's

Deutsche Mythologie in Teplitz in 1843. Through Peter Cornelius he was also able, with some difficulty, to borrow the Imperial Library's copy of Johann Christoph Wagenseil's Nuremberg Chronicle (*De Sacri Rom. Imperii libera civitate Norinbergensi commentatio*, Altdorf, 1697). From the latter, in particular, he derived the detail (already mentioned as appearing in Text II) of the ancient art of *Meistergesang* of which he made so much use in the opera; Wagenseil's influence, detailed and far-reaching, is most conveniently dealt with separately (see Chapter 3). Grimm's book, his first published work, contributed an idealised vision of Mastersong, Nuremberg and Hans Sachs to the newly aroused delight in the German past shared by the first generation of Romantics. Among them was E. T. A. Hoffmann, whose works Wagner read eagerly. He had made a draft for an opera for Josef Dessauer on Hoffmann's *Die Bergwerke zu Falun* in Paris in 1842, and another of his favourite works, to which he returned for readings with Cosima in later years, was *Signor Formica*. The story may well have given him the idea of an old man serenading a young girl, and its ludicrous aspect. Of greater significance, though, was the story *Meister Martin der Küfner und seine Gesellen* (1819). Hoffmann had also read Grimm, and his tale evokes a charming picture of old Nuremberg and a society in which 'artists and artisans, hand in hand, march happily together towards a common goal'. Adam Puschmann is mentioned, and the Mastersingers Hans Vogelgesang and Heinrich Frauenlob, together with some of the quaintly named modes, and St Sebald's Church; and finally, after morning service in St Catherine's, there is a song-trial with a competition between two young men, Reinhold and Friedrich. Friedrich has returned to Nuremberg, and confesses to Master Martin's beautiful daughter Rosa that he became a cooper so as to be able to make an approach to her. Reinhold delights the Mastersingers with songs on different modes, even though one or two of his listeners find that he has a foreign manner they cannot quite understand; but when Friedrich mounts the stand, and, having looked about him and cast his gaze upon Rosa, sings a song to one of Heinrich Frauenlob's tones, 'the Masters declared with one voice that no-one among them was the equal of the young man'. (Other composers were to set the story as operas, among them, perhaps surprisingly, Wendelin Weissheimer, who had a close if equivocal relationship with Wagner during the time of the composition of *Die Meistersinger*. Bizet also contemplated a setting.)

Possibly Wagner also knew *Norika*, the so-called *Nürnbergische Novellen aus alter Zeit* by August Hagen (Leipzig, 1827). Popular enough in its day to have earned an English translation in 1851, this is a set of sketches of old Nuremberg supposedly based on an ancient tome discovered by Hagen in the library of the Königsberg Hochschule. The city is lovingly described, with copious references to its buildings and monuments, and to distinguished inhabitants such as Albrecht Dürer. Outside St Sebald's, the writer comes upon a commotion, and is told that an important meeting of the Mastersingers is about to take place in honour of the visit of the Emperor Maximilian. There follows a description of a Trial, complete with the solemn entry of the Masters, of the Tabulatur, and of the *Gemerk* or dais for three Markers; two of these note errors in prosody and in Biblical reference, while the third acts as secretary. Hagen makes use of Wagenseil's names for some of the Masters, including Konrad Nachtigall, who makes a muddle of his song about the Heavenly Jerusalem. Fritz Kothner fails even to get properly under way on the Creation before he is 'out-sung'. Eventually old Linhard Nunnenbeck takes the stand and, with his song on a theme from the Apocalypse, delights one and all, none more than his proud pupil Hans Sachs. He is awarded the prize of a silver chain with a medallion representing King David.

However, there is the ever-present danger, with an artist who drew so much into his imagination as Wagner, of assuming that whatever preceded him and then occurs in some form in his operas was of necessity used by him or influenced him; in fact little or nothing occurs in *Norika* that Wagner could not have got from elsewhere. Quite a number of unlikely sources for incidents in the opera have been put forward. Charles Malherbe and Albert Soubies, for instance, suggest in their *Mélanges sur Richard Wagner* (Paris, 1892) that there is an influence to be found in a one-act operetta by C. Luce-Varlet entitled *L'élève de Presbourg*, which was produced at the Opéra-comique on 24 April 1840. Wagner was in Paris, and could have seen it, despite his claim to have gone to the opera very little during his years in the city; but its tale of rivalry between the young Joseph Haydn and an old Italian pedant named Rondonelli for the daughter of the Austrian Imperial Kapellmeister Kreisler has more in common with Pushkin's fictional rivalry between Mozart and Salieri than that between Walther and Beckmesser, despite the love interest absent from Pushkin. By the same token, there seems little reason in suggestions that Wagner took hints from Dekker's *The Shoemaker's Holiday* (1600). The plot is entirely different, and the character of Simon Eyre, the cheerful, eccentric cobbler who becomes Lord Mayor of London, has no real affinity with Sachs. Nevertheless, there is possibly a trace of the much-despised August Kotzebue to be found in Act II of *Die Meistersinger*. His play *Die deutsche Kleinstädter* of 1802 long remained popular, and was responsible for putting into common parlance the notion of 'Krähwinkel' as a tiny, backward-looking, artistically complacent town epitomising all that was stagnant in German provincial society. In the fourth act, the ludicrous lover Sperling leans out of an upper window, accompanying with a violin his own serenade to a girl who is not, as he supposes, opposite him but locked in the arms of her lover below. The neighbours are roused to protest, and noisy arguments ensue, to be quelled by the nightwatchman with lantern and horn singing the old couplet used by Wagner (and, for that matter, by Mendelssohn before him in *Die Heimkehr aus der Fremde*),

> Hört ihr Herren und lasst euch sagen:
> Die Glocke hat neun geschlagen.

Wagner was prepared to take a good idea from anywhere, though he did not always care to acknowledge it.

Certainly he was familiar with some of the work of the Director of the Vienna Court Theatre, Johann Ludwig Deinhardstein. There is probably no more than coincidence in the central use, in *Salvator Rosa* (1823), of the device whereby an old lecher is duped. The wealthy Calmari hopes to woo his ward Laura, who is in love with the young painter Ravenna. Calmari goes to Salvator Rosa and asks to buy an unsigned painting which he can then pass off as his own so as to impress Laura. Rosa gives him one by Ravenna, promising that he will never lay claim to it; and the discovery of its true authorship leads to a happy ending for the lovers. The trick seems enticingly close to Wagner's own with Sachs and the Prize Song; but it must be remembered that Wagner had two attempts at solving this problem in Text I and only found the answer in Text II, so that without evidence that he had seen or read *Salvator Rosa* between 1845 and 1861 (which is possible), we should assume that he reached the answer by working it out for himself.

However, Wagner knew Deinhardstein's *Hans Sachs* (1827), which he had seen at the age of fourteen and encountered afresh through Lortzing's opera of 1840. The plot can be summarised as follows.

The young Hans Sachs is in love with Kunegunde, daughter of the rich jeweller Steffen, who disapproves of him as a mere artisan. But Sachs is proud of his calling, and will not change it. Steffen favours instead the absurd young Eoban Runge, a foppish councillor from Augsburg who turns up in time to catch Sachs with Kunegunde and create a scene. In Act II, Eoban needs some shoes and orders them disdainfully from Sachs. Kunegunde pretends to agree to drop Sachs if it can be shown that he is really nothing more than a mere cobbler. But when she presses him to give up his trade, he breaks from her and decides to leave Nuremberg. In Act III, he meets on the road, but does not recognise, the Emperor Maximilian, an admirer of his poetry. Sachs guides him to Nuremberg. Steffen has been elected Burgomaster, he believes on the influence of Eoban. He presses Eoban on Kunegunde, who still loves Sachs and refuses. Sachs intervenes, and resists the order of the magistrate to let her go. In Act IV, the Emperor steps in to release Sachs from arrest: Eoban is routed, the lovers receive both paternal and Imperial blessing, and Sachs wins the crown for his poetry.

Deinhardstein was a writer of moderate gifts, and not only is the framework of the plot stiff, but the characters who fill it are also limply characterised. Steffen and Eoban are no more than types, Kunegunde hardly better, and Sachs has a negligible degree of fantasy or originality in his make-up; while the device of *imperator ex machina* is a feeble one with which to bring about the dénouement. But the play provided the material for Lortzing's 1840 opera, whose librettists Philipp Reger and Philipp Jakob Düringer added a number of ingredients, ideal for Lortzing's vein of robust humour and simple characterisation. Eoban (now with the surname Hesse) becomes another poet, who arrives in Nuremberg with the intention of joining the Mastersingers' Guild. Steffen secretly arranges for the Markers to proclaim Eoban victor in a song contest, then announcing that he will give Kunegunde to the winner. In Act II, Eoban is proclaimed the winner, despite popular support (and that of Kunegunde) for Sachs. Meanwhile, Sachs's apprentice Görg, in love with Kunegunde's cousin Kordula, has passed off as his own a poem by Sachs which he has stolen. When the emperor hears it, he demands to know the author. Görg is afraid to claim it, so Eoban suggests to the Masters that he himself claims it. But when he is made to recite it, he forgets it and muddles it up with an absurd poem, *The Death of Absalom*, with which he defeated Sachs in Act I. Görg is forced to confess, and all ends happily.

There are in *Die Meistersinger* features unique either to Deinhardstein's play or to Lortzing's opera which point to Wagner's knowledge of them both. Deinhardstein responds to the suggestions of the historical Sachs as a dreamer by making him see the Muse of Poetry crowning him with a laurel wreath; and Sachs is also shown as a poet of independent cast of mind who scorns the Masters' rules and Tabulatur. In Lortzing, as well as one striking musical similarity between Görg and Wagner's David (Ex. 1.1), there is the device of a gathering of the citizens of Nuremberg and a sequence of dances before the dénouement: Wagner's Paris experiences were scarcely needed for him to turn this into a *Festwiese* scene powerfully shaped by the example of Grand Opera.

Example 1.1

Wagner must also have known Goethe's prologue, written for the Berlin production of the play in 1828, which includes a poem entitled *Erklärung eines altes Holzschnittes, vorstellend Hans Sachsens poetischen Sendung*. In 184 lines it sketches a highly rhetorical picture of the old cobbler-poet, wise and level of judgement, gazing one Sunday morning on a vision of a torn and confused world, consoled by the affection surrounding him and inspired by his devotion to poetry. Wagner also knew, since the book was in his Dresden library, Friedrich Furchau's *Hans Sachs* (1820), an imaginative account that includes several suggestions which may have contributed to his own portrait of Sachs. On his travels as a young man, Sachs rises 'nach kurzem Schlafe und lieblichen Träume' ('after a brief sleep and some delightful dreams'); and one of his most important poems is a disputation on love between 'Der Alter' ('the old man') and 'ein Ritter stolz' ('a proud knight'). Whether or not this is the origin of Walther von Stolzing's name, the account of the poem is interesting for showing Sachs's independence of mind.

> Sachs warf die todten und müheseligen Regeln bei Seite, liess den Eingebungen und Erfindungen seines Geistes und dem aufgeregten Herzens-Drange und Kummer freien Raum und es entstand folgendes Gedicht, was er schon damals am ersten Mai 1515 in seinen zwanzigsten Lebensjahre wörtlich also niederschrieb, als das früheste und erste aller seiner übrig gebliebener Gedichte.

> (Sachs threw aside the dead and burdensome rules, gave free rein to the inspiration and invention of his spirit and the aroused impulse and grief of his heart, and there came into being the following poem which he wrote on the first of May 1515 in his twentieth year as the earliest and first of all his poems.)[16]

Much later, Sachs is described sitting on a fine Sunday morning in his workshop writing *Die Wittembergisch Nachtigall*. Furchau's book is a *Künstlerroman* of the kind immensely popular in those years: the genre took as its main inspiration Goethe's *Wilhelm Meister* (*Künstlerroman* as well as *Bildungsroman*), and included Ludwig Tieck's *Franz Sternbalds Wanderungen* (1798). It is not an example of much distinction, but apart from its incidental details it perhaps interested Wagner for its example of an imaginative treatment of an artist possessing insight, no less valuable than a factual account. This was, indeed, one element in the complex attraction that drew him to the most important influence on his characterisation of Sachs, discussed in Chapter 4, that of Arthur Schopenhauer.

On 2 December 1861, Wagner read the new draft to Schott in Mainz, and managed to extract ten thousand francs from him. Having asked Schott's wife Betty on the 10th to obtain a book of German folk-songs and Protestant chorales, he set off for Paris to begin work on the libretto in earnest. An offer of accommodation from Princess Metternich having fallen through, he was obliged to take a room at 19, Quai Voltaire, where he settled down in reasonably good humour. A letter of the 15th to Minna shows that he was making progress, though not in chronological sequence: he had worked out Walther's Trial Song, Sachs's reflections on it (with the last four lines of the *Flieder* monologue), and Eva's reaction to the 'Morning Dream Song'. His first letter to Mathilde includes a passage in which he seems to apologise for his failure to appreciate the works of art they saw in Venice, adding that he saw only inward pictures needing expression in sound. On Christmas

Day, Mathilde wrote to him sending the old *Meistersinger* sketch of 1845. She had re-read it, and found it excellent, she told him, hoping that he might make use of some of the many promising ideas in it. She adds that she had dared not hope for so much when they were in Venice, which further suggests – since he was not likely to have kept his thoughts about himself from her – that the Titian 'revelation' had grown in his memories. At the end of December he wrote acknowledging the sketch, in a letter filled with expressions redolent of 'Freund Schopenhauer' (to whose work he had introduced her) and evidently resigning himself to renouncing her. He signs himself, as he often did, 'Der Meister', and appends three verses of Sachs's cobbling song, explaining the references to Eve (Eva in German) with a note, 'Eva is also the name of the young girl who has just decided to elope with her beloved.' It is the first direct reference to the Eva/Eve connection that was to be so fruitful. A note to the Wesendonks of about 1 January, though initialled R.W., wishes them 'Viel Glück' for the New Year from 'Hans Sachs', and on 3 February he reproaches Mathilde for not writing, quoting Pogner's words to Eva, 'Und du, mein Kind, du sagst mir nichts?' ('And you, my child, do you say nothing to me?').[17] The MS, made between 25 and 31 January, is a fair copy from Text IV, whose three acts were written on 5, 16 and 25 January.

As it happens, he had some trouble with one couplet of the third verse of the cobbling song, concerning the angel calling Sachs to Paradise. The verse begins:

> O Eva! Hör mein Klageruf,
> mein Not und schwer Verdrüssen!
> Die Kunstwerk', die ein Schuster schuf,
> sie tritt die Welt mit Füssen.
> Gäb nicht ein Engel Trost,
> der gleiches Werk erlost,
> und rief mich oft ins Paradies,
> wie ich da Schuh und Stiefel liess!

> (O Eva! hear my lament,
> my trouble and heavy vexation!
> The works of art a cobbler made,
> the world treads them underfoot!
> If an angel did not give comfort,
> one whose lot has been the same work,
> and who calls me often into Paradise,
> how readily I would abandon shoes and boots!)

There then follows, in Text IV, under a heavy deletion:

> Doch küsst der Engel mir die Stirn,
> dann schall ich Werke für das Hirn.
>
> (But when the angel kisses my brow,
> The work I make is for my brain.)

Dissatisfied with this, he made some other attempts in the left-hand margin, including one rhyming 'hält' with 'erhellt', which perhaps he realised might have cost Sachs four marks in a song trial under the category of *Aequivoca*. Finally, in the right-hand margin, he settled for:

> Doch wenn der mich im Himmel hält
> dann liegt zu Füssen mir die Welt.
>
> (But when he bears me up to Heaven
> the world lies at my feet.)

This is the version in Text V and in the opera. Clearly Wagner has sensed that he could improve upon the comparatively plain comparison of handwork and brainwork, and has worried away at the text until he hit upon the stronger poetic idea of the cobbler whose work the world treads under its feet now finding, as poet, the world at his feet. As it happens, the historical Sachs was less scrupulous: in his poem *Die ungleichen kinder Eve* of 25 August 1546 (marked to be sung in the *Frauenlob* tone) he includes the rhyme of 'schon' with 'edelmon' (dialect for 'edelmann'), specifically forbidden in the Tabulatur as a *Laster* and earning a penalty of two points. Wagner adds several other references to the poem, conveying his exhilaration at what he was doing, in a few more notes and letters from Paris to Mathilde, to whom he was to give this draft after making the fair copy (Text V).

Text IV, the first draft of the complete poem, is filled with such evidence of his mind at work. It covers sixty-eight unnumbered pages, written with some evident haste but in the same bold hand that he refined for his fair copy (Text V). There are no serious changes in structure or dramaturgy between the two texts, but a good deal is altered, some with heavy or even indecipherable crossings-out and extra passages scribbled in the margins. He must also have used and destroyed scraps of paper to work out the sometimes elaborate verses, since these are often written down in their final form; but in a good many cases one can see at work a process that did not stop with minor revision when he copied out Text V nor even with the first printing of the libretto before he set the words to music. He claimed that in Paris, away from a piano, he was only writing the words; but it is inconceivable that, given his approach to his work, he would not have had some idea of the kind of music he was intending and for which he was forming the text. Moreover, there were moments when a musical idea came to him, as with the opening music for 'Wach' auf' (*Die Wittembergisch Nachtigall*), which he said occurred to him as he arrived at a café and for which he demanded a piece of paper. On the other hand, there are many alterations to the text which show how musical needs came to override more strictly poetic considerations. 'Simultaneity' in the composition of words and music was for Wagner an extremely complex and subtle process, alternating and interacting, the poetic or musical aspect of the idea conditioning and sometimes correcting the formation of the other.

A first and obvious feature of Text IV is the absence of the opening chorale; and the idea for this came to Wagner so late that even in Text V it is written in the margin with an arrow to show the place of its insertion ([X] in the following quotation): 'On the rise of the curtain there is heard, with organ accompaniment, the last verse of a chorale on which there ends the afternoon service [before St John's Day], sung by the congregation. [X] During the chorale and its intervening music [*Zwischenspiele*] there develops the following pantomime.' The mention of St John's Day first occurs in Text V, but there is no indication as to what he intended, and the insertion of the chorale verse is not intercalated into the pantomimic exchanges between Eva and Walther. The text is a paraphrase of a hymn by Luther set more than once by Bach, as Wagner knew, and also familiar to him from a book in his Dresden library, K. E. Philipp Wackernagel's *Das deutsche Kirchenlied von Martin Luther bis auf Nicolaus Herman und Ambrosius Blaurer* (Stuttgart, 1841):

Luther	Wagner
Christ, unser Herr, zum Jordan kam	Da zur dir der Heiland kam,
nach seines Vaters willen,	willig deine Taufe nahm,
Von S. Johans die Taufe nahm	weihte sich dem Opfertod,
sein werck und ampt zurfüllen.	gab er uns des Heils Gebot:
	dass wir durch dein' Tauf' uns weih'n
	seines Opfers wert zu sein.
	Edler Täufer! Christs Vorläufer!
	Nimmt uns gnädig an,
	Dort am Fluss Jordan!

This example alone would show how Wagner's ideas continued to grow, not only between the two Prose Sketches of autumn 1861 (Texts II and III) but throughout the writing of the poem and, indeed, even after its printing and then during the composition of the music. Close comparison of the two MSS, the first printed text, and the score, discloses many significant differing points of detail, as well as a number of substantial alterations (some of these

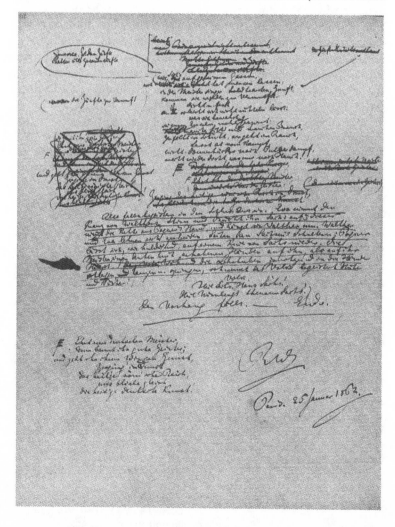

Plate 1.1 The closing page of the first draft of the libretto, 25 Jan. 1862.

are pointed out in Egon Voss's valuable essay introducing a facsimile of Text V, *Richard Wagner: Die Meistersinger von Nürnberg*, Mainz, 1983). One of the most crucial developments concerns the *Wahn* monologue itself. The first part of the monologue is virtually identical, up to the account of the madness possessing people: 'Mann, Weib, Gesell und Kind, fällt sich an wie toll und blind!' ('Man, woman and child attack one another as if mad and blind'). From here to the end, Wagner has rethought his ideas, as can be seen in the comparison in Appendix I. It looks as if he realised, when he came to compose the text, that music could more effectively achieve what the omitted (and perhaps too insistently Schopenhauerian) lines about the glow-worm attempt, and that by reordering the couplets he already had at his disposal, the expression of destructive disarray could be attached to mankind earlier in the text and the idea of the bereft glow-worm be left poetically oblique.

The matter of Sachs's final address is still more complicated. The opening in Text IV, Sachs's defence of the traditions of Mastersong down to 'Was wollt ihr von den Meistern mehr?' ('What more do you want of the Masters?') has comparatively few alterations or second thoughts. Wagner then went on with a version arrived at after many deletions and revisions in Text IV (see Plate 1.1, Wagner's fair copy and revision as Text V in Plate 1.2, and the transcription and translation of the latter in Appendix II). It can be seen that he has some trouble at the start of the passage beginning 'Gewerke, Gilden und Zünfte, hatten üble Zusammenkünfte', eventually preserving only that couplet in Texts IV and V. He then continues with few changes down to 'macht wieder dicht, was nur noch Hauch!' Then follows the quatrain:

> Rühme der deutsche Krieger
> Besiegter oder Sieger:
> Ehrt ihr die deutschen Meister
> dann werd ihr Herr der Geister.
>
> (Honour the German warrior,
> vanquished or victor:
> praise the German Masters,
> and you shall command the spirits.)

This was struck out, the first couplet permanently; but the second was retained, with further attempts at improving the second line, to begin the section worked out on the left of the page, and then fair-copied at the bottom of the page.

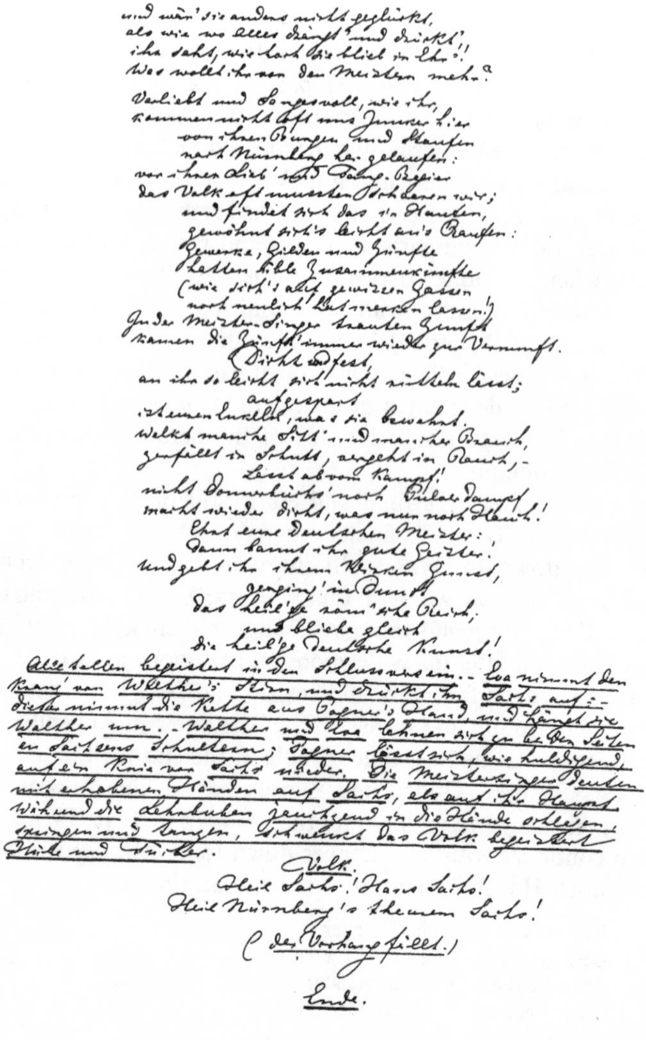

und wär' sie anders nicht geglückt,
als wie wo Alles drängt' und drückt',
ihr seht, wie hoch sie blieb in Ehr'!!
Was wollt ihr von den Meistern mehr?

Verliebt und Sangesvoll, wie ihr,
kommen nicht oft uns Junker hier
von ihren Burgen und Stauffen
nach Nürnberg hergelaufen:
vor ihrer Lieb' und Sang-Begier
das Volk oft mussten flüchten wir;
und findet sich das in Haufen,
gewöhnt sich's leicht an's Raufen:
Gewerke, Gilden und Zünfte
hatten üble Zusammenkünfte
(wie sich's auf gewissen Gassen
noch neulich hat merken lassen!)
In der Meister-Singer trauten Zunft
kamen die Zünft' immer wieder zur Vernunft.
Dicht und fest,
an ihr so leicht sich nicht rütteln lässt;
aufgespart
ist Euren Enkeln, was sie bewahrt.
Welkt manche Sitt' und mancher Brauch,
zerfällt in Schutt, vergeht in Rauch, –
Lasst ab vom Kampf!
nicht Donnerbüchs' noch Pulverdampf
macht wieder dicht, was nur noch Hauch!
Ehrt eure deutschen Meister:
dann bannt ihr gute Geister!
und gebt ihr ihrem Wirken Gunst,
zerging' in Dunst
das heil'ge römische Reich,
uns bliebe gleich
die heil'ge deutsche Kunst!

Alle fallen begeistert in den Schlussvers ein. – Eva nimmt den Kranz von Walther's Stirn, und drückt ihn Sachs auf; dieser nimmt die Kette aus Pogner's Hand, und hängt sie Walther um. – Walther und Eva lehnen sich zu beiden Seiten an Sachsens Schultern; Pogner lässt sich, wie huldigend, auf ein Knie vor Sachs nieder. Die Meistersinger deuten mit erhobenen Händen auf Sachs, als auf ihr Haupt hin, und die Lehrbuben jauchzend in die Hände schlagen, springen und tanzen, schwenkt das Volk begeistert Hüte und Tücher.

Volk.
Heil Sachs! Hans Sachs!
Heil Nürnberg's theurem Sachs!

(Der Vorhang fällt.)

Ende.

Plate 1.2 The closing page of the fair copy of the libretto, 31 Jan. 1862.

However, Wagner's difficulties were not over. During the composition of the music, he decided that the long passage in Texts IV and V held matters up; and it does indeed add little that music could not provide and smacks rather too much of a sermon. By 1867, he was even considering abandoning the whole address and ending on Walther's Prize Song. It was Cosima who 'pulled a face', she told King Ludwig, and persuaded him to think again. On 28 January he recast the address, abandoning everything but the last seven lines and prefacing them with the contentious passage warning against the threat to 'deutsches Volk und Reich', and that if 'wälsche'[18] customs should invade Germany, then no Prince would know his people and the people themselves would not know what was 'deutsch und echt'. At the time, the passage (which places stress on the Mastersingers' arts of peace as crucially distinct from politics or war) would have seemed to no-one any more objectionable as an expression of love of country and anxiety about foreign threat than John of Gaunt's speech about England in *Richard II*; and it is only in the light of the then-distant future horrors of German nationalism that it has caused distaste.

The question of the Prize Song is even more fundamental. From Biebrich (whither he withdrew from Paris to compose the music), Wagner wrote to Mathilde on 12 March 1862 to tell her of a successful reading of the text to the Grand Duke, and saying, 'You lack the melody of Walther's song, which is inevitably the most important part. I've written the verses after the melody in my head: that of course you couldn't imagine. But just hear how easily it flows [Ex. 1.2]. The people hear only the melody of the whole thing: guess my secret who can.'[19] As far as the 'secret' is concerned, it is possible that the similarity of the melody to the two *Wesendonklieder*, 'Der Engel' and 'Stehe still', which Wagner wrote to words by Mathilde, indicated that here was a homage to her; but the melody is not so distinctively associated with them as to support this contention, and the words are more connected to maternal love than to the elective affinity he felt for her.

More to the point, in any case, is the imaginative shift which led Wagner, even after the printing of the text, to change such a crucial element in the opera. As with the earlier linking of the opening chorale with St John's Day, Hans Sachs's name day, so the Eva/Eve connection had strengthened and grown. At the same time, he may have felt that something radically different from 'Am stillen Herd' was advisable: the two share a compound time metre, and there are certain turns of phrase in common also with 'Fanget an!'. On 28 September 1866 he drafted the new melody of the Prize Song, bringing, out of the melody in the Overture associated with youthful ardour, the final *Abgesang* that crowns Walther's triumph. Not until 24 December did he find the words (which do

32   Die Meistersinger von Nürnberg
Example 1.2

not fit all that well); and the MS (included in a five-leaf folio, Text VII) shows, with its many deletions and revisions, that he had trouble with it. The abandoning of the Dream Song was a constructive move. Its narration of a young man leaving his home, inspired by his mother's tender care to seek life and love, with the white dove of Faith carrying a branch from the Tree of Paradise, is quite nicely turned, but it has none of the connecting resonances of the Prize Song. It survives, otherwise inexplicably, into Sachs's mention of a dove that has led Walther's servant in his wake to Nuremberg with his wedding garments: was Wagner also remembering Gervinus's comparison of Sachs himself to a dove? The rewriting naturally involved Wagner in a new version of Beckmesser's distortion of the song in the *Festwiese*, which is faintly pencilled over the draft of the Prize Song in Text VII; but he also seized the opportunity for an inspired stroke in the opera. Originally, he intended to save the third verse of the Dream Song for the *Festwiese*, but not introduce alterations; now, he makes an extra point about creative freedom when, to avoid such repetition, he has Kothner, overcome with emotion, drop his copy of the song and so allow Walther new flights of creative fantasy. In both songs, Wagner has written the music before the words. Times have changed since *Oper und Drama*.

There is another connection which resolves the emotion in the *Abgesang* of the Prize Song as well as further indicating the constant evolution of Wagner's ideas. In Text IV, near the start, Walther bids farewell to Eva, as Magdalene drags her away from the church, with the promise that if he cannot win her by the sword he will do it by song. Wagner then added in the margin couplets for Walther and Eva and a comment from Magdalene:

WALTHER:	Für euch Leben und Blut! Für euch dichtende Mut!
	(For you life and blood! For you poetic ardour!)
EVA:	Mein Herz, seliger Glut! für euch liebender Flut!
	(My heart, blissfully glowing for you, with love flowing!)
MAGDALENE:	Schnell heim, sonst geht's nicht gut!
	(Home, quick, or there'll be trouble!)

From the quintuple rhyme divided between the three of them, it seems likely that Wagner meant them to make a strong cadence together; but when he came to write the music, he found such a beautiful way of contriving it from the theme in the overture that metrical niceties were well sacrificed (Ex. 1.3). There are many other instances throughout the opera where musical demands overrule the original wording, metre and even rhyme; and there are naturally very many additions and deletions. In Text IV, the Apprentices' baiting of David is added, and it was another after-thought to have them open Act II with their singing of 'Johannistag!'. Copious alterations show that Wagner had a good deal of trouble with the Song Trial scene and even more with the Riot scene; and both Dream Song and Quintet caused difficulty.

The substitution of the Prize Song for the Dream Song does weaken the connection between Sachs's lesson in his workshop and its expression in Walther's song, and with it an extra emphasis on the idea of art as associated with dreams. Wagner had clearly been impressed with Schopenhauer's belief that whereas the dreams

Example 1.3

experienced in deep sleep cannot be remembered, and represent an unconscious inaccessible to the conscious mind, those experienced shortly before waking are formed by the unconscious but remain in the conscious mind on waking – what Schopenhauer calls 'a light morning-dream to one half-awake, through which reality already shines'.[20] The morning dream is thus seen as constituting an intermediary between the unconscious and the conscious. Schopenhauer later writes, 'The search for a recollection shows itself in a peculiar way, when it is a dream that we have forgotten on waking up. Here we look in vain for that which a few minutes previously occupied us with the force of the clearest and brightest present, but has now entirely vanished. We then try to seize any impression that has been left behind'.[21] He further suggests that such dreams have a close connection to the artistic process, in that they are unwilled manifestations of the deepest wells of the mind which can nevertheless be taken up by the exercise of the conscious mind.

This is of course the substance of Sachs's lesson. Walther arrives in Sachs's room, having slept 'ein wenig, aber fest und gut' ('a little, but soundly and well'), and having experienced a beautiful dream which he scarcely dare tell for fear of losing it. Sachs replies that this is precisely the poet's task, that man's 'wahrster Wahn' ('truest illusion' does not give the full resonance of the phrase) is disclosed to him in dreams, and that all poetry and versifying is nothing but true dream-interpretation. Sachs goes on to make a comparison between the instinctive impulses of creative youth and the difficulty of retaining these in later life; hence, he advises, the value of artistic disciplines, such as had been formulated by the Mastersingers in early days (he further points out) to preserve a pristine image in later, troubled times. He encourages Walther to relate his morning-dream, saying that to preserve it he needs poetic art ('Dichtkunst'); and when Walther asks if what he experienced was then not dream but poetry, Sachs replies that the two are close friends. This leads fluently into the original Dream Song, which in detail confirms and is confirmed by all that Sachs has said (see Appendix III).

However, Sachs's instruction does not really need such detailed confirmation. Quite apart from the quality of the verse, and the associated musical inspiration, the Prize Song serves to focus more important metaphors illuminating the opera. Biblical allusions suffuse a work which, from the opening chorale, is deeply imbued with the Lutheran spirituality and morality which Hans Sachs so strongly represents. He himself, as David remembers in his ditty about the Nuremberg woman turning up on Jordan's bank, is named Hans after John the Baptist. He is the one who can with authority follow Mastersinger custom and baptise the new song with its name, 'Die selige Morgentraum-Deutweise' ('The Blessed

Morning-Dream Melody'). Walther first seems to Eva like David – not, that is, the crowned King on the Mastersingers' banner but the young David ready to topple Goliath, as depicted by 'Meister Dürer'. Eva herself acquires a Biblical name, one with which she is repeatedly associated. She is the 'schlimmes Weib' ('wicked woman') of Sachs's ironic song, whose expulsion along the hard road from Eden set the angels cobbling for her and Adam. She is also the mysterious woman who in the first verses of the Prize Song inspires the singer, showing him fruit on the Tree of Life and laurels on another tree; and in the *Festwiese* she is revealed as both the Muse of Parnassus and Eve in paradise.

Throughout the work, both additions and deletions can be revealing. Sachs's important lines urging the Mastersingers, 'So lasst das Volk auch Richter sein' ('Let the people also be the judge') were only arrived at after several attempts. Wagner's continuing doubts about Sachs's moral position in allowing Beckmesser to make use of the Prize Song are suggested by the late addition of the couplet, 'Die schwache Stunde kommt für jeden, Da wird er dumm, und lässt mit sich reden' ('The hour of weakness comes to everyone, Then he looks foolish and takes counsel with himself'). Sachs himself has previously reflected that Beckmesser cannot keep his malice up and must retain some reason: the addition proposes that the hour of weakness, when Beckmesser is exposed, will reveal him to himself, and that this is therefore constructive for Beckmesser as well as helping Sachs's plan. It can hardly be denied that there is a degree of moral sophistry here.

Apart from the numerous deletions of words and sometimes lines, there are several passages with some import which Wagner eventually dropped. Voss points out three of the most significant which are to be found in Text V. In Act I, Sachs originally was to add, to his proposal for the people to choose once a year, four lines suggesting that there should also be a public Song Contest in which, although the rules must apply, anyone could enter with a song to a subject of his own choice in his own style. Perhaps Wagner felt that this would have provoked an even louder uproar, and one inconvenient to handle musically in a section that remains somewhat protracted in the opera. Also to be deleted was a less significant quatrain in which Kothner emphasises to Walther that he must be properly instructed in song and verse if he is to be considered for election to the Guild. And later, there was originally a longer passage in which Sachs points out that in Walther's answer to their questions with 'Am stillen Herd' he has made a correct bar of Mastersong: he gets support from Vogelgesang for the *Stollen* and from Nachtigall for the *Abgesang*, with Kothner dissenting over the melody. Among other alterations is the insertion of the action for Beckmesser as he starts to leave Sachs's room with the Prize Song, rushes back thinking he has forgotten it, and eventually makes off. Perhaps Wagner felt he needed more music to make the transition at this point, as well as to emphasise Beckmesser's shoddy behaviour.

Wagner completed Text IV in Paris on 25 January 1862, and made the fair copy (Text V) between 25 and 31 January. It was from this that he read the poem at Schott's in Mainz on 5 February and at the Grand Duke's in Biebrich early in March. Text IV he gave to Mathilde, and Text V was handed over to Schott for printing after Wagner had made another copy (or more likely had one made by a copyist: this, Text VI, is now lost). Then on 23 November came the reading in the house of his friend Dr Joseph Standhartner in Vienna, to which he had disingenuously invited Eduard Hanslick. Wagner and he were by now on poor terms, and Hanslick had doubtless got wind of the fact that the Marker had originally been named Hanslich. However, he came, and perceived the kind of posterity Wagner was planning for him. It says much for his dignity that he seems to have confined his reactions to taking his leave without comment.

2 Synopsis

Hans Sachs, shoemaker		(bass)
Veit Pogner, goldsmith		(bass)
Kunz Vogelgesang, furrier		(tenor)
Konrad Nachtigall, tinsmith		(bass)
Sixtus Beckmesser, Town Clerk		(bass)
Fritz Kothner, baker		(bass)
Balthasar Zorn, pewterer	Mastersingers	(tenor)
Ulrich Eisslinger, grocer		(tenor)
Augustin Moser, tailor		(tenor)
Herman Ortel, soap-boiler		(bass)
Hans Schwarz, stocking-weaver		(bass)
Hans Foltz, coppersmith		(bass)
Walther von Stolzing, a young Franconian Knight		(tenor)
David, Sachs's apprentice		(tenor)
Eva, Pogner's daughter		(soprano)
Magdalene, Eva's nurse		(soprano)
Nightwatchman		(bass)

Burghers of all Guilds, journeymen, apprentices, girls, people

Nuremberg, about the middle of the sixteenth century

It is well known that Wagner composed the prelude before the rest of the opera, and included in it no reference to Hans Sachs. It does, however, like each of Wagner's mature preludes, include many of the opera's other most important elements: he was later to insist that his preludes had to be *elementarisch*. In some instances, melodies are completely formed, and later find further realisation in the opera: such is the melody which becomes the *Abgesang* of the Prize Song (Ex. 7.16). More significantly, the opening theme and its fanfaring answer (Exx. 7.3, 7.4), redolent of the grandeur, the self-importance and the sense of honour and tradition associated with the Mastersingers, is destined to play the most important of all thematic roles in the entire opera, deriving as it does from one of the *Vier gekrönte Töne* and generating so much of the invention. Not least, the antithesis of the innovative and the traditional is foreshadowed, including the contrapuntal working between them which is to be a characteristic of the opera's invention. Wagner has seized on some of the opera's creative elements before all the characterisation that embodies them is fully formed. The principal missing element is the idea of *Wahn* that was to transform Sachs from an ironic observer into one of Wagner's most profound and sympathetic characters. Wagner's account of the Prelude's inception is typical.

During a beautiful sunset which transfigured the light as . . . I contemplated a splendid view of "Mainz the Golden" and the majestic Rhine streaming past it, the prelude to my *Meistersinger*, just as I had once seen it as a distant apparition rising from a mood of despair, now returned clear and distinct to my soul. I set about putting the prelude on paper and wrote it down precisely as it is in the score today, with all the main themes of the drama definitively formed. From there I went on in the text, working on the ensuing scenes consecutively.

Wagner's creativity frequently extended to his memory. It is not true that he was suddenly inspired to write out the prelude as it now stands: his sketchbooks include more than a dozen different fragments of it, and the first draft shows many changes and corrections. Not for the first or last time, the idea of inspired creator was more attractive as public 'image' than that of patient craftsman, perhaps particularly in view of the subject of the opera to come.

Act I

SCENE I   In St Catherine's Church, Eva and her nurse Magdalene are sitting in the congregation as morning service is finishing with a chorale ('Da zu dir der Heiland kam'): the melody (Ex. 7.5) is Wagner's own, derived from the *gekrönte Ton*. Walther von Stolzing, newly arrived in Nuremberg and visiting Eva's father Pogner, is trying to attract her attention, with contrasting phrases that pick up the key theme of the chorale's falling fourths and rising scale in beseeching tones. Eva distracts Magdalene sufficiently to enable him to ask if she is betrothed. But Magdalene overhears, and any answer is interrupted by the appearance of her own betrothed, David, to a diminution of the Mastersingers' theme (Ex. 7.3). In any case, Magdalene explains, Eva is promised to the Mastersinger who wins a prize in the song competition at the Feast of St John on the morrow. To Magdalene's embarrassment, Eva bursts out

that this will be Walther or no-one. David has by now come to
set up the rostrum and curtains for a singing trial, in which an
apprentice may succeed in becoming a Mastersinger. His own
theme (Ex. 7.21) appears as Eva goes on to compare Walther to
David: at first Magdalene takes this to mean her own David, then
supposes that Eva means the Biblical musician-king David on the
Mastersingers' banner; but Eva explains that what she has in mind
is the younger David who slew Goliath (as perhaps Walther may
overcome his towering adversaries). Walther resolves to enter the
trial and win Eva.

SCENE 2   As other apprentices begin to set up the singer's chair
and the marker's box for the trial (which at first they do incorrectly for a *Singschule* rather than a *Freiung*), David explains the
rules to the bewildered Walther: who the Marker is, how he calls
'Begin!' to the postulant, what is the difference between the various
grades of poet, and then how the Mastersingers' rules of poetry
are applied and finally, with many graphic illustrative touches,
what is the nature of the variously named Tones that must be
learnt: all this is closely modelled on the *Tabulatur* (see Chapter 3).

SCENE 3   The Mastersingers begin to assemble. Pogner first enters
in company with Beckmesser, assuring him of support in the
coming contest, which he will surely win; but Beckmesser is
unhappy about the clause allowing Eva, though she must choose a
Master for husband, to decline the winner if she wishes. Pogner
agrees to speak for him. Walther approaches Pogner with his wish
to become a Mastersinger; Pogner is delighted, but Beckmesser,
observing the stranger, is immediately suspicious. This long
dialogue, conducted over reiteration and development of a simple
figure and in light orchestration, as befits two old friends engaged
in private conversation, is interrupted by a bar's rest. The Mastersingers have been gathering, Hans Sachs last of all: it is time for
the junior Mastersinger, Kothner, to call the roll. This he does,
over continued reiteration and development of the previous figure,
and in growing fullness of orchestration, as the Mastersingers
gather and answer according the formal requirement of the Guild.
But before they can proceed to the election of the Marker, Pogner
begs leave to speak. In what is generally known as Pogner's Address
he begins, to the 'Johannistag' music (Ex. 7.20), 'Das schöne Fest',
by reminding them of the Feast and its atmosphere of holiday as

the people pour into the meadow outside the town and listen to the Mastersingers' trial singing. Pogner, as a rich man, has been pondering what to give as a prize: he goes on, in troubled music, to lament how on his travels he has found the burghers to be held in such low regard for their meanness, despite their devotion to art. So his gift to the winner of the trial is to be his only daughter, Eva. This causes a sensation among the Mastersingers, expressed in some of the most contrapuntally active music so far heard; Sachs reflects that some men would give up their wives for Eva. Pogner adds that Eva must have the casting vote, irritating Beckmesser and giving Kothner cause for concern that she will be overruling the Mastersingers' decision. But Pogner insists that though she can refuse the winner, she can only choose a Mastersinger for husband; and Sachs suggests that there is a case for letting the people's voice be heard beside hers. He does not calm the Mastersingers' agitation by further suggesting that the rules should be tested by popular acclaim from time to time, and annoys Beckmesser by declaring that Eva's wooer must be younger than either of them. Walther is now summoned by Pogner, and steps forward to the knightly theme (Ex. 7.23) which dominates the ensuing discussion as to whether or not he is eligible; when Sachs points out that his rank is irrelevant, he is asked to justify himself by declaring his artistic lineage. He answers with a three-stanza statement ('Am stillen Herd'), first how he learnt in the depths of winter by studying Walther von der Vogelweide, then how he learnt from the birds in springtime on the Vogelweide, and finally how all his experience will lead him to produce a Mastersong. Though Vogelgesang has noticed the quality of the opening two stanzas, Beckmesser is irritated, Kothner puzzled, and only Sachs tolerant. To a measured version of Ex. 7.3, the Marker's box is made ready, and as Walther opts for a secular theme, Beckmesser (to Ex. 7.22) enters the box with the dry reminder that only seven faults will be allowed. To developments of Ex. 7.3, Kothner recites the *Tabulatur*. When Beckmesser calls 'Begin!' ('Fanget an!), Walther echoes 'Fanget an!' as the first words of his Trial Song in praise of spring beginning the year's cycle by releasing the world from winter (developing towards the climactic Ex. 7.1). Beckmesser's busy scratchings do not deter Walther from proceeding with another section, then returning to the opening music as he compares spring with the awakening of love in his heart. Beckmesser interrupts with a slate covered in chalk marks, and points to all the alleged errors. Only

Sachs finds interest in what to the other Mastersingers seems chaos, and, having come close to quarrelling with Beckmesser over the Marker's personal animosity towards a rival, urges Walther to continue. Walther sings of a wonderful bird soaring above the envious crows and daws, in an increasingly elaborate musical texture. The Masters fall to arguing among themselves while he sings on, to the admiration of Sachs. He finishes and storms out, followed by the apprentices and then the Mastersingers, leaving only Sachs, pensive but finally turning away with a humorous gesture of discouragement.

Act II

SCENE I   On one side of a narrow alley stands Pogner's fine house by a lime tree, on the other Sachs's simpler house under an elder. The apprentices are shutting up shop, singing of next day's Midsummer Feast ('Johannistag'). Magdalene comes out of Pogner's house with a basket of food; she asks David how Walther fared, whisking the basket away and disappearing when the news is bad. Sachs interrupts and sets David to work indoors.

SCENE 2   Pogner and Eva come down the alley. He is uncertain about asking Sachs's advice, following their disagreements that morning. Eva refuses to speak, and (to suggestions of the theme associated with Nuremberg, Ex. 7.18) nervously listens to her father's pleasurable anticipations of the Feast next day when she will choose her bridegroom. Eva responds with relief to Magdalene's beckoning in to supper, waiting until Pogner has gone indoors to learn, to her distress, of Walther's failure but also that Magdalene has a plan.

SCENE 3   Sachs tells David to move the cobbling stool into the open and to go to bed. Seated under the elder, he begins his *Flieder* monologue ('Was duftet doch der Flieder'). The scent relaxes him, tensed as he is by the song he heard that morning and ready to give up poetry for his cobbling; yet the song will not let go of his mind, even though he cannot work it out; it had no rule, yet no fault; it was so old, yet so new, like the Maytime birdsong it celebrated; it came from spring's command (Ex. 7.2); the bird that sang today had a well-formed beak, he ends, and if it displeased the Mastersingers, it greatly pleased him.

SCENE 4   Eva appears, and in a long dialogue with Sachs reveals her anxiety about Beckmesser winning her hand. She has known Sachs as child and as woman: perhaps he might claim her. Sachs does not rise to this, pleading that his brain is in turmoil as a result of the song trial at which Walther had failed. He leads Eva on by suggesting that this knightly upstart could never succeed; when she flares up and storms across to her own house at Magdalene's summons, his suspicions are confirmed and he resolves to find a way to help the lovers. He conceals himself where he can observe Magdalene telling her that Beckmesser is to serenade her that night. They plot to seat Magdalene, anxious at having upset David, at the upper window so that his jealousy will be aroused by the serenade while Eva can meet Walther below.

SCENE 5   Eva greets Walther (now using the intimate 'du' form of address). He is depressed at his failure, and with it the impending loss of Eva, and launches into a long tirade against the Mastersingers. He is interrupted by the Nightwatchman sounding his horn and intoning an old German call for the hour of ten. But Sachs has overheard the lovers' plan to elope, which he must prevent. When Eva emerges from her house in Magdalene's dress and they turn to leave, they are suddenly caught in a shaft of light which Sachs directs across the alley.

SCENE 6   Beckmesser now appears, and begins to tune his lute. Walther turns his wrath from Sachs to Beckmesser, but is restrained by Eva, and they conceal themselves as Sachs prepares to work on Beckmesser's shoes for the Feast. As Beckmesser is about to sing, Sachs begins a cobbling song ('Jerum, Jerum') to a vigorous hammering theme. To Beckmesser the singing is an unwelcome interruption, to Walther an unwelcome delay; but Eva is pierced by the words. They tell of Eve being driven from paradise, tramping her hard road, and an angel being set to cobble shoes for her and Adam, so that she has it on her conscience that a man must cobble; and he continues that the world treads his work underfoot until he reaches heaven, when the world lies at the feet of Hans Sachs, cobbler but also poet. Magdalene, in Eva's clothes, now opens the upper window. Beckmesser strikes a bargain with Sachs: he will sing, and Sachs will mark any mistakes with his hammer so that shoes and serenade may both proceed. Beckmesser is soon interrupted by hammer-blows, and at first pauses to argue poetic niceties with Sachs. However, he continues in the face of Sachs's increased hammering until he has finished his second verse and Sachs has finished the shoes. His third verse begins to rouse the neighbours, including David, who, on seeing Beckmesser serenading the house in which Magdalene lives, falls upon him.

SCENE 7   Other neighbours join in, and quarrels spring up among them as a mindless riot develops (based chiefly on Ex. 7.19 and fragments of Beckmesser's serenade), with townsfolk, journeymen and apprentices finding the occasion to settle old scores; even the Masters begin to take part in the fighting. Magdalene tries in vain to restrain David, and Pogner pulls her back from the window. As Walther now tries again to elope with Eva, Sachs restrains him, pushes Eva into her house, and drags David and Walther into his. Beckmesser limps away and the crowd swiftly disperses on hearing the Nightwatchman return sounding his horn and singing his call for the hour of eleven, to a now empty alley in the moonlight.

Act III

SCENE 1   The Prelude opens with a full statement of the melody associated with *Wahn* on strings, followed by a sonorous statement of the chorale later to be sung to Luther's poem 'Wach' auf'. The following morning, Sachs is seated in his workshop absorbed in a large book. David appears with a basket of food and flowers. He nervously reports having delivered Beckmesser's shoes, and prattles on seeking forgiveness for his part in last night's riot without gaining Sachs's attention. Finally Sachs closes his book with a bang, startling David to his knees. Sachs is a little absent, still absorbed in thoughts of the riot, but questions David about the basket and asks to hear his poem. David begins by singing it to the tune of Beckmesser's serenade, but is quickly pulled up by Sachs. He resumes (Ex. 7.6) with his song about St John baptising, in the River Jordan, people from all lands including a Nuremberg woman's son, named John but back in Nuremberg known as Hans. This reminds him that today, Johannistag, is Sachs's name-day, so he tries to give his master the contents of his basket. Sachs refuses, and also refuses to go wooing when David suggests it, declaring that time brings wisdom. David leaves in some puzzlement. In his *Wahn* Monologue ('Wahn! Wahn!'), Sachs reflects on the world's folly, on the riot, and on his resolve to turn this destructive *Wahn* to nobler ends.

SCENE 2 Walther appears, having dreamt a wonderful dream. Sachs tells him that man's truest *Wahn* is disclosed in dreams, and the poet's task is to interpret this; and he assures the dubious Walther that it is still possible to convince Mastersingers who may be confused by disturbing experiences but are men of honour. He adds that to sing when young is one thing, but to preserve art when older demands mastery; the Mastersingers' rules must be learnt early, for they had been formed so as to preserve what was good. Walther dictates to Sachs the first verse of his Prize Song ('Morgenlich leuchtend in rosigem Schein': Ex. 7.7): he has dreamt of being welcomed on a beautiful morning into a garden. Sachs encourages him to give this *Stollen* a partner: in the garden stands a beautiful tree. Finally there must be an *Abgesang* so that the pair have a child: by the tree stood a beautiful woman pointing towards the fruit of this Tree of Life (Ex. 7.16). Sachs is moved by the completion of this *Bar*, even though he finds the melody rather too free. Walther goes on with a second *Bar*: in the evening he has lain taking inspiration from her eyes, as two stars shine through the branches, and then, as a spring murmurs, more stars gather like fruit in the laurel tree. They agree to wait for the third *Bar* until the right moment, and go off to change for the Feast.

SCENE 3 Beckmesser, finely dressed but bruised and shaken, limps into the shop, peers through the window, hobbles about (obsessed by his memories of the riot, as a complex of motives recalls). He finally lights upon the Prize Song, in Sachs's handwriting. He pockets it when he hears Sachs returning, and complains about his shoes; then he bursts into a rage against Sachs for having plotted to humiliate him and win Eva for himself. When Sachs denies it, Beckmesser produces the Prize Song; Sachs makes him a present of it, warning him that it is difficult. Though delighted, Beckmesser is suspicious and makes Sachs promise that he will never claim authorship of the song. He hurries away, leaving Sachs reflecting on this useful turn of events for his plan.

SCENE 4 Eva enters, dressed in white. She is nervous, and alleges that her shoe pinches (to developments of Ex. 7.9); when Walther enters, also dressed for the Feast, she is transfixed (Ex. 7.10), and Sachs understands why she is here. He removes the shoe, and pretends to work at it while grimly reflecting he must always cobble away and not follow up her own suggestion of wooing her.

Walther sings the third *Bar* of his Prize Song: the stars of his
dream were in the woman's hair, her eyes were like twin suns, as
she poured love into his poet's heart. Eva bursts into tears, and
casts herself on Sachs's breast; he composes himself, and, giving
her to Walther, rages against his lot as always having to cobble
everything together for everyone else, whether shoes or poetry
(Ex. 7.11), with young girls exploiting his good nature when in the
end he is considered no more than a coarse workman. He is about
to go in search of David when Eva stops him with a cry of love,
reminding him (Ex. 7.12) how much she owes him in teaching her
of life, how if she were free she would choose him. Sachs quotes
the tale of Tristan and Isolde (to a musical quotation from *Tristan*):
he does not want to play King Mark, and has escaped that by
finding the right man for her. Magdalene and David now appear,
also dressed for the Feast, and Sachs declares that they must,
according to custom, baptise the Prize Song. First, he makes David
a journeyman with the traditional box on the ear, then names the
Prize Song 'The Blessed Morning Dream Interpretation Melody'.
They celebrate it in the Quintet ('Selig, wie die Sonne': Ex. 7.13):
Eva dwells on her hopes for the Prize Song winning her; Walther
dreams that the melody born of love and sung in this room
may win the highest prize before the Mastersingers; David and
Magdalene find their own dreams of his promotion and their
marriage are close to realisation; while Sachs, almost unnoticed in
the texture of the music, reflects that he must subdue his longing
to speak his heart to Eva, and that the song reminds him that the
green shoots of youth are only kept fresh through the craft of
poetry. They leave for the Festival Meadow.

SCENE 5   In the Festival Meadow outside the city gates, parties
of burghers from the Guilds, with their wives and families, are
arriving in boats off the River Pegnitz, welcomed and led in procession to their places by the Mastersingers' apprentices. A stand
with benches has been set up, and the guild banners are placed
there. First come the Cobblers, singing of their patron Saint
Crispin and how he would steal leather to make shoes for the
poor. Next come the Tailors, with their story of the tailor who
saved Nuremberg by frightening off besiegers when he dressed up
in a goatskin as the Devil. They are followed by the Bakers,
singing of famine averted by their craft. To the delight of the
apprentices, a boatload of girls from Fürth arrives; the Dance of

the Apprentices with the girls is joined by David, once he is assured that Magdalene is not looking. He is interrupted by the Entry of the Mastersingers (Exx. 7.3 and 7.4), led by Kothner as standard-bearer, and followed by Pogner leading Eva with Magdalene, then the other Mastersingers. Last of all comes Hans Sachs. When they see him, the people greet him with his own poem, 'Wach' auf', sung to a Lutheran chorale (of Wagner's invention). His response is a memory of *Wahn*, and he replies, at first in halting phrases, that he is done too much honour; his address will speak of the honour to art for its own sake, and he tells of the rich Mastersinger who is to give the highest of all prizes, his daughter in marriage, for the sake of art, to the winner of the song contest. Moved, Pogner thanks him. He turns to Beckmesser, who has been having difficulty memorising the Prize Song and is counting on Sachs's popularity to win the song success. The apprentices have made a little mound of turf, and Kothner calls on him, as eldest, to take this stand first. Especially when he slips climbing onto it, the people mutter and laugh among themselves. Kothner calls on him to begin. He garbles the words ludicrously in a feeble and mis-accentuated melody, to the puzzlement of Mastersingers and people which then turns to mocking laughter. Beckmesser furiously declares the song to be by Sachs and rushes off. Called upon to explain, Sachs declines the honour of having written the song, which in any case needs singing correctly, and summons Walther to prove it, giving Kothner the copy. Walther takes the stand, and begins his first *Stollen*; but when Kothner lets fall the copy, he changes the words to name the beautiful woman as Eve in paradise. People and Mastersingers are much affected now that the song is sung aright. Walther's second *Stollen* now names the woman as the Muse of Parnassus. His listeners are deeply moved, and he continues to a conclusion in which he claims to have won Parnassus and paradise. He is acclaimed by all, though it is the people and not the Mastersingers who do so first, and take up his own melody. Eva, also claiming Walther with his melody, crowns him with laurel and myrtle, and kneels with him for Pogner's blessing. But when Pogner bids him welcome into the Guild (to Ex. 7.4), he rejects it. Sachs strides forward and (combining Ex. 7.3 and Ex. 7.7, tradition and innovation) orders him not to scorn the Mastersingers: it is not his ancestry but his artistry that has won him Eva, artistry cared for down the years by the Mastersingers. The times are dangerous, he continues, and if their land were to fall to foreigners it would be in art that what is German and true would survive; so he should honour the Mastersingers, since if even the Holy Roman Empire were to pass away, German art would remain. Walther now accepts the Mastersingers' chain. As Eva crowns Sachs with the laurel, they all take up his last words and acclaim him.

3   Sachs, Beckmesser and Mastersong

As we have seen, Wagner's first known encounter with the Mastersingers and their art came with his reading of Gervinus in 1845; this was followed in 1861, when he resumed work on the text for the opera, with study of Jakob Grimm's *Ueber den altdeutschen Meistergesang*, of Furchau's life of Hans Sachs, and then of Wagenseil's history of Nuremberg, when he was able to persuade Cornelius to get it for him from the Vienna library (the copy, still held there, is free from any revealing markings, which may disappoint researchers but speaks for Wagner's proper respect).

The art of *Meistergesang* arose in various German cities during the fourteenth century, and consisted of the composition of *Meisterlieder* by *Meistersinger*. The Mastersingers were generally drawn from a town's professional classes and artisans, who would unite in a guild; the Guild of Mastersingers was unique in drawing its members from the whole range of these trade guilds (Wagner alludes to this in a passage deleted from Sachs's final address: see Appendix II). It was rare to find among them a member of the aristocracy, hence the surprise of Wagner's Mastersingers at Walther von Stolzing's application, and the need for Sachs to remind them that 'ob Herr, ob Bauer, hier nichts beschliesst' ('whether gentleman or peasant is not here at issue').

There seems to have been a good deal of common ground between the rules agreed upon in different cities, encouraged no doubt by trading exchanges and by the experiences of young men travelling in search of fortune and adventure. The poets who enjoyed these carefree *Wanderjahre* earlier in the Middle Ages included, as their most famous name, Walther von der Vogelweide (*c*.1170–*c*.1230), the *Minnesinger* whose love poetry set a new standard in its freedom from courtly convention (though not enough of his music has survived for real evaluation). His poems

49

and those of his fellows gave both example and encouragement to the guilds in the cities. The poems of the *Minnesinger* were love songs with complex stanza structures, originally derived from the patterned verse of the Provençal troubadours. The subject is complex, and continues to be one of scholarly debate, but it seems agreed that *Bar* form (simply expressed, A–A–B) became common around the beginning of the thirteenth century. Other features included sometimes beginning a song with a description of nature or the time of year (which survives in Walther von Stolzing's 'Am stillen Herd' from his studies of Walther von der Vogelweide) and the increase, especially among the early *Meistersinger*, of elaborate melismata (which survive as a satirical archaicism in Beckmesser's songs). After the Reformation, vernacular religious poetry played an increasingly important role in educating the public from the singer's rostrum as well as in church. There had always been a strong moral element in the German art of song, as befitted the position proudly held by those who had earned professional as well as artistic recognition in their city, and this was developed in support of the Reformation's tone of moral fervour. At the same time, an honourable place was still accorded to love songs. The most significant single Mastersinger, who produced traditional love poetry but also worked and wrote to put into artistic and popular currency the language of Luther's translation of the Bible and the substance of his teaching, was Hans Sachs.

It is from the Nuremberg guild of Mastersingers that the greatest amount of information has survived. Among the singers of the period were the baker Konrad Nachtigall (*fl. c.*1410–*c.*1485, first documented in Nuremberg in 1436) and the nail-maker Fritz Zorn (*fl.* 1441–7); other important Mastersingers of this early generation were Lienhard Nunnenbeck, a weaver who was Sachs's teacher, and the surgeon-barber Hans Folz (1435 or 1440–1513), who became a citizen of Nuremberg in 1459. However, it was the example of Hans Sachs (1494–1576) that gave the Nuremberg guild particular renown and influence beyond the confines of the city. His contemporaries included Hans Vogel and, among others whose names can be found in records or whose work has survived, Adam Puschmann.

A Silesian born in Görlitz in 1532, Puschmann had travelled in his *Wanderjahre* in search of towns where Mastersong was cultivated. His life's work was to bring honour back to the art. He settled in Nuremberg, where he was a pupil 'bey dem sinnreichen

Hans Sachs', on whom he published an obituary essay, *Elogium reverendi viri J. Sachs* (1576). He died in 1600. His *Gründtlicher Bericht des deudschen Meistergesangs* (Görlitz, 1571) consists of thirty quarto pages, giving an example of the Tabulatur and listing twelve 'famous men': 'Herr Walther ein Landtherr von der Fogel weid, Wolfgangus Rohn ein Ritter, Marner ein Edelmann, Doctor Frawenlob, Doctor Mügeling beyde Doctores Theologiae, Magister Klingessohr, Magister Starcke Popp, und fünff Bürger, mit namen Regenbogen, Römer, Cantzler, der alter Stoll und Conradus von Würtzburg'. These are cited as the first Masters. When Wagner's Walther claims as his teacher the first of these, Walther von der Vogelweide, he is already declaring an imaginative connection with the very origins of the art, which Beckmesser, in reply to Sachs's respectful 'ein guter Meister', fails to understand with his literal-minded retort, 'Doch lang' schon todt'. Walther is further connected by Wagner to a strong image that runs through the opera, that of the bird as natural singer: his exemplar Walther is 'von der Vogelweide'; when he tells how he learnt from finches and thrushes, it is Kunz Vogelgesang, otherwise with little to say, who speaks up in praise of his two *Stollen* (and in a second admiring intervention, deleted from Text V in the opera, was joined by Konrad Nachtigall); in the original Prize Song (see Appendix I) there is the pervasive imagery of a white dove; Sachs, seated beneath the *Flieder*, reflects that the song, 'so old and yet so new', was like 'Vogelgesang in süssen Mai', sung by a bird with a finely formed beak. There are other pervasive allusions, perhaps at their back the image of the 'wonnige Nachtigall' associated by the historical Sachs with Luther in the poem with which, in the opera, he is hailed by the populace. This is specifically invoked in the closing section of Walther's 'Am stillen Herd', where the dark birds of night are dazzled by 'ein Vogel wunderbar' that soars on golden wings into the light; though the inspiration is here not religious but artistic, with the lurking nocturnal creatures associated not with the Roman clergy but with the pedantic Masters, the imagery is similar.

Puschmann relates the evolution, out of much dissension, of a single *Tabulatur*, whose role was in part to arrest a decline that had begun to affect the art. He also gives the rules for a *Schulordnung*. His book copies melodies from *Schulbücher*; it is not a direct source, which would have to be a *Schulbuch* made at the time, and though there are one or two scattered later MSS, no notated melodies survive from the earliest Mastersong. However,

Puschmann is the best surviving source, and was the obvious one
for the most famous early work on the Mastersingers of Nuremberg,
and the one that most influenced the relevant detail of Wagner's
text, that by Johann Christoph Wagenseil, published at Altdorf in
1697. It is entitled, in full, *Joh. Christophori Wagenseilii de Sacri
Rom. Imperii libera civitate Norinbergensi commentatio. Accedit, de
Germaniae phonascorum von der Meister-singer origine, praestantia,
utilitate et intitulis, sermone vernaculo liber* (The commentary of
Joh. Christoph Wagenseil on the free city of Nuremberg in the
Holy Roman Empire. To which is added a book in the vernacular
on the origin, standing, usage and customs of the singing-masters
of Germany, the Mastersingers). Wagenseil's Commentary is, for
the most part, a history and description of Nuremberg in Latin
(interlarded with quotations and translations in German, French,
Greek and Hebrew). It is rambling and somewhat unfocussed,
though it includes some interesting illustrations: among these is a
pictorial map of the city, folded into the end of the book, which
includes representation of the churches of St Martha (where the
Mastersingers used to meet in Sachs's day) and of St Catherine
(where Wagner eventually set their meeting). The long section on
the Mastersingers is separately entitled *Iohann Christoph Wagenseils
Buch von Der Meister-Singer Holdseligen Kunst, Anfang, Fortübung,
Nutzbarkeiten, und Lehr-Sätzen. Es wird auch in der Vorrede von
vermuthlicher Herkunfft der Ziegeiner gehandelt* (Johann Christoph
Wagenseil's book of the Mastersingers' noble art, its origins, practice, application and rules. There is also in the preface treatment
of the supposed origin of the gypsies).

Wagenseil's attempt to identify gypsies with German Jews and
to connect them with the Mastersingers is a predictable failure;
and there is little point in his setting out of a conversation on
irrelevant topics with the French novelist Madeleine de Scudéry.
Presently he begins to discuss the *Spruch-Sprecher*, versifying
orators who would attend weddings and other functions; but he is
careful to distinguish between these humble hirelings, seeking only
a fee and a good meal, and the Mastersingers. His account of the
origin of the latter is deeply suspect, and depends upon such
assumptions as a piece of false etymology trying to connect the
word 'bard' with the *Bar* used by the Mastersingers (Puschmann
had suggested *par*, from the Latin for 'equal'). His 'twelve famous
men', rather different from Puschmann's, arrived at the art 'as if
by divine revelation' when the Mastersingers themselves were 'in

einem sehr irrigen Wahn' ('under very false illusions': the word 'Wahn' does not as yet carry its later philosophical overtones). These Masters flourished at the time of Otto I, and the poem which records their names gives the date as 962. They are Heinrich Frauenlob, Heinrich Mögeling, Nicolaus Klingsohr Meister der freyen Künste, Der starcke Poppo, Walther von der Vogelwaid, Wolfgang Rohn oder Rahm, Hanns Ludwig Marner, Barthel Regenbogen, Sigmar der Weise, Conrad Geiger, N. Cantzler, and Steffan Stoll. Two of these names will of course immediately strike the Wagnerian. One is, again, Walther von der Vogelweide; and the other perhaps struck Wagner himself since Wagenseil describes at length the successful defence of the pious Wolfram von Eschenbach against the assaults, in a contest at Eisenach, of the evil Klingsohr and his black arts. Wagner had, of course, already come upon mention of Clingsor in 1840 in his reading of Wolfram's *Parzifal*. Wagenseil rightly points out that there was a certain amount of myth in these names since Frauenlob, described in 'an old poem' held in honour by the Mastersingers, is placed three centuries too early – as is, of course, Walther von der Vogelweide. (It may be that Wagner also noticed mention of one Petrus Paganus from Wanfried, in Niederhessen.)

A number of different singing schools are known to have existed, including those in Augsburg, Freiburg-im-Breisgau, and Strassburg (or Strasbourg: Wagenseil draws attention to the local Mastersingers' success, during French rule, in preserving *Hochdeutsch* secure from, as Wagner was to put it, 'wälschen Dunst mit wälschen Tand'). In the time of which Wagenseil wrote, the mid sixteenth century, meetings were held only on Feast Days, in St Catherine's Church between mid-day and Evensong: Markers, or *Vorsteher*, had to send out invitations, conveyed by the junior Mastersinger. At the meeting, all the names were read out, and attendance was compulsory except in the case of illness. A *Singschule* was public, and was announced on four or five different placards (one at least displaying King David playing his harp). There were four Markers, one comparing the verse with Luther's Bible, a second checking against the *Tabulatur*, a third observing the rhymes, and a fourth concentrating on the *Ton*. There was also a *Schulhalter*, a supervisor or umpire. The others had to keep silence. The singer had to sit on the chair, remove his hat, greet the Masters and bow. The Marker would call, 'Fanget an!', afterwards 'Fahret fort!'. After all had sung, the Masters conferred, and the best singer became the

Davidsgewinner, or *Übersinger*. The prize was a long silver chain with medals, though its cumbersomeness later led to a cord with silver medals being substituted. The runner-up was awarded a wreath of silk leaves. The Marker was enjoined to score 'treulich und fleissig nach Inhalt und Kunst, nicht nach Gunst' (faithfully and diligently according according to the subject and the art shown, not according to his own taste). At the meeting afterwards, quarrelling was forbidden.

The wish to order and discipline artistic practice led in time to the sets of rules that were, by the sixteenth century, codified in *Tabulaturen*. The *Schulordnungen* (School regulations) established by these provided the basis for the songs performed both in private *Zechsingen* (friendly, relaxed occasions held in taverns: *Zech* is the word for the bill in an inn, hence *Zecher*, a drinker) and before the public in the *Singschulen*. In the Nuremberg of Sachs's time, the regular practice seems to have been for the twelve senior members to elect three Markers. A *Singschule* was usually held once a month on a Sunday, after the morning service, in one of the city's churches. At the main performance, or *Hauptsingen*, only scriptural songs were permitted; during this solo performance, the Markers sat inside their cubicle, or *Gemerk*, deciding on the basis of their *Tabulatur* whether the song was correct according to the doctrines and language of Luther's Bible, and further whether text and music obeyed the given rules of prosody and composition. The singer with the fewest errors was awarded a silver chain hung with medallions, the largest of which portrayed the Mastersingers' patron, the musician-king David. Luther himself was to draw attention to the curing of Saul's melancholy by David as witness of the healing and strengthening power of music as a moral force. A set of conventions governing competitive singing in late-medieval German cities had clearly, by the mid sixteenth century, been given new life by the moral energy and popular enthusiasm of the Reformation.

Wagenseil goes on to list twelve Nuremberg Mastersingers of the Reformation: Veit Pogner, Cuntz Vogelgesang, Hermann Ortel, Conrad Nachtigal, Fritz Zorn, Sixtus Beckmesser, Fritz Kohtner, Niclaus Vogel, Augustin Moser, Hanns Schwartz, Ulrich Eisslinger and Hanns Foltz. Wagner's only alteration to this list, apart from details of spelling, and allowing Vogel to be absent through illness, is to rechristen Fritz Zorn with the more resounding name Balthasar. His later attempt to pillory Hanslick by naming the Marker as Veit Hanslich seems the more perverse when there was at hand the name of Sixtus Beckmesser, with its hissing, cutting sounds and indeed its associations of 'knife'. Wagenseil goes on to give an account of the life and career of Hans Sachs, claiming that he had so stimulated the art of Mastersong that in his time there were over 250 Mastersingers in Nuremberg, and that he left over 4,370 Mastersongs, as well as volumes of poetry, which earned him a place in the memory of the people beside Homer, Virgil, Ovid and Horace.

Hans Sachs was, in fact, born in Nuremberg on 5 November 1494. He went to school in the city, and then learnt the trade of a cobbler. Between 1511 and 1516 he pursued his *Wanderjahre*, travelling widely though without leaving German lands. He then settled in Nuremberg, where he had already joined the guild of Mastersingers, becoming a master cobbler in 1520. More than any other Mastersinger, he was responsible for associating Mastersong with the Reformation, in his songs, his poems and prose dialogues, his dramatic comedies and tragedies. He composed thirteen *Meistertöne*, of which the most famous was the *Silberweise*. He married twice: his first wife, Kunigunde Kreuzer, whom he married in 1519, bore him two sons and five daughters, all of whom predeceased him; she herself died on 18 March 1560. At the age of sixty-six, on 2 September 1561, he remarried, his new bride Barbara Harscher being a widow of 29. She brought into his house six children from her first marriage, which was to a candlemaker named Enders. Sachs was thus a widower for only two summers, in one of which the opera is presumed to be set (Wagner also left a sketch for a drama about his second marriage). He died on 19 January 1576.

From Wagenseil and from Grimm, Wagner would have learnt more than these bare facts about one of the most remarkable artists of the Reformation. Sachs was only twenty-eight when he first came to know Luther's writings. Immediately sympathetic, he spent all his spare time studying the theological controversies that were rending Germany. In 1523, after a long silence, he wrote the poem in honour of Luther entitled *Die Wittenbergisch Nachtigall*. Luther, who had taught at Wittenberg and there, in 1517, nailed his famous theses to the door of the Schlosskirche, is conceived of as the nightingale voice which draws into safe pastures the sheep who have strayed from their neglectful pastors into the regions of the devouring lion (the Pope) and wolves (the Roman clergy), with their adherent geese, frogs, foxes and serpents. It is Luther's song which awakens the flock from night and turns it to the true light. The poem mocks the excesses of the Roman Catholic Church and the corruption of the clergy, satirises the sale of indulgences that had been the object of Luther's first great attack, denounces Papal luxury and hypocrisy, and ends with a great call for a return to Christ's teaching (see Plate 3.1).

It was an inspired gesture of Wagner's to take the first eight lines of this tremendous poem as the people's salutation to Sachs himself as he enters the Festwiese.

> Wach auf, es nahet gen den Tag,
> ich hör' singen in grünen Hag
> ein' wonnigliche Nachtigall,
> ihr' Stimm' durchdringet Berg und Tal:
> die Nacht neigt sich zum Okzident,
> der Tag geht auf vom Orient,
> die rotbrünstige Morgenröt'
> her durch die trüben Wolken geht.

> (Awake, the day is drawing near,
> I hear, singing in the green grove,
> a wonderful nightingale,
> its voice rings through hill and dale:
> the night is sinking in the west,
> the day breaks in the east,
> the ardent rosy glow of morning
> shines through the clouds.)

The real impact was, initially, very different. Sachs's poem is remarkable for its range and vigour of expression, for its force of conviction, for its inspired tone. The City Fathers of Nuremberg took fright: the cobbler was summoned to appear before them, and invited to stick to his last. His personal popularity saved him from harsher measures. Soon afterwards, the Council was to follow Sachs into the Lutheran camp; meanwhile, his poem had spread across Germany as a clarion call on behalf of the Reformation. Wagner would have been well aware of these resonances when, setting it to a Lutheran chorale of his own invention, he placed it as he did in his opera. He is hardly likely to have read more than cursorily in Sachs's voluminous writings, some of which are marked by the moralising but also the light irony often commented upon as among his characteristics. In Sachs's plays, the classical gods and heroes are diminished by being clothed in local colour (Agamemnon brings his wife Clytemnestra some presents back from Troy, as if

Die Wittenbergisch Nachtigall
Die man yetz höret vberall.

Ich sage euch/wa dise schweygē/so werden die stein schreyē Luce. 19.

Plate 3.1 Contemporary woodcut illustrating Hans Sachs's poem 'Die Wittenbergisch Nachtigall', captioned, 'Ich sage euch/wa dise schweygen/ so werden die stein schreyen' ('I tell you that, if these should hold their peace, the stones would immediately cry out') (Luke 19, v 40).

to placate her after a lengthy business trip); and the figures taken from German mythology are hardly more admirable. The death of Siegfried, in *Sewfriedt*, is seen as little more than an obstreperous boy's reward for shameless, impulsive behaviour that takes no account of moral considerations; and *Tristan* reminds us of the dangers of irregular liaisons. It is possible, however, that Wagner noticed Sachs's drama of the repentant Eve, or the poem in which her children are given their allotted ranks in society by a God who explains to her that this is His will for order.

With his fifth chapter, Wagenseil comes to the *Tabulatur*. Several examples of *Tabulatur* survive, but Wagenseil's is by far the most extensive and detailed, based as it is on a comparison of a number of versions. It is introduced with a sonorous call to order (the original punctuation slashes are retained):

Das jeweil alle Kunst/darinnen sich der Mensch übet eine ordentliche Anleitung haben muss/nach welcher sich die Schüler derselbstigen Kunst üben müssen/so lang/biss sie von Tag zu Tag/je länger je baass/den rechten Grund und Verstand ihrer angefangenen Kunst ergreiffen mögen/so sol und muss auch die hochlöbliche Christliche und holdselige Kunst des Teutschen-Meister-Gesangs/welches erstlich/durch hochverständige und wohlgelehrte Leute/als Doctores Ritter und Freyherrn/Edle/und andere verständige Leute/Reich und Arm/ist erfunden worden/einen gründlichen Bericht haben/damit die Tichter/Mercker/und Singer/sich darinnen ersehen/ und erfahren mögen/was der rechten wahren Kunst Ordnung sei. Und dieweil auch viel und mancherley Singer und Tichter seyn/welche etwan aus guten verständigen Worten und Meinungen eine Ungunst machen/ also ist für nöthig erachtet worden/die rechte Artickel und Tabulatur dieser Kunst/wie sie von ihrer alten Erfindern auf uns herkommen/zu erklären/damit man spüren/verstehen und erkennen kan/was sträfflich oder unsträfflich/was zu loben/oder zu schelten sey.

(As every art with which man is concerned must have an ordered rule according to which the students of this art must exercise themselves so that they can from day to day, and the longer the more effectively, grasp the correct foundation and understanding of their chosen art, so shall and must even the most praiseworthy Christian and gracious art of German Mastersong, which was evolved by the most intelligent and learned men, such as doctors, knights, nobles, gentlemen and other men of wisdom both rich and poor, possess a fundamental code to which poets, markers and singers can refer and learn what the ordering of the right and true art may be. And as there also exist many and various singers and poets who perhaps regard wise words and views with disfavour, it has been thought necessary to set forth the correct articles and tablatures as they have been communicated to us by their ancient inventors so that one may judge, understand and comprehend what is culpable or without fault, and what earns praise or blame.)

There follows a passage 'Von der Meister-Gesangs wie auch deren Art und Eigenschafften' ('On Mastersongs, and their art and characteristics'). *Bar*, it should be remembered, was the term (not always used correctly by Wagner) which the Mastersingers gave to a whole song: it was always in AAB form, with an uneven number of stanzas.

Ein jedes Meister-Gesangs Bar hat sein ordentlich Gemäs/in Reimen und Sylben/durch des Meisters Mund ordinirt und bewehrt/diss sollen alle Sänger/ Tichter/und Mercker auf den fingern auszumessen/und zu zehlen wissen. Ein Bar hat mehrenteils unterschiedliche Gesätz oder Stuck/als viel deren der Tichter tichten mag. Ein Gesätz bestehet meistentheils aus zweyen Stollen/die gleiche Melodey haben. Ein Stoll/bestehet aus etlichen Versen/ und pflegt dessen Ende/wann ein Meister-Lied geschrieben wird/mit einem Kreutzlein bemerckt werden. Darauf folgt das Abgesang/so auch etliche Vers begrifft/welches aber eine besonders und andere Melodey hat/als die Stollen.

(Every Mastersong Bar possesses its own proper metre in rhymes and syllables, ordered and approved out of the Master's own mouth so that all singers, poets and markers know how to count them on their fingers and calculate them.

A Bar is usually composed of several sections or parts, as many as the poet may compose. A section usually consists of two Strophes having the same melody. A Strophe consists of various lines of verse, and its conclusion, when a Mastersong is being written, is usually marked with a small cross. There then follows the Aftersong, consisting of several couplets but with an individual and different melody from that of the strophes.)

Wagner's skill in fashioning this to his own use – and thereby making an implicit point about the artist turning even the recitation of dry rules to poetic ends – can be observed when he puts these sentences into Kothner's mouth for the reading of the *Tabulatur* in Act I, scene 3:

Ein jedes Meistergesanges Bar
stell' ordentlich ein Gemässe dar
aus unterschiedlichen Gesätzen,
die keiner soll verletzen.
Ein Gesätz besteht zus zween Stollen,
die gleiche Melodei haben sollen;
der Stoll' aus etlicher Vers' Gebänd',
der Vers hat seinen Reim am End'.
Darauf so folgt der Abgesang,
der sei auch etlich' Verse lang,
und hab' sein' besondre Melodei,
als nicht im Stollen zu finden sei.

Wagenseil now proceeds to give an example of a Bar, with two *Stollen* making up the *Aufgesang*, then the *Abgesang*:

Aufgesang
Wer seine Hoffnung hat auf Gott gesetzet
Derselbige wird nicht zu Spott
Ja dessen Glaub niemalen wird verletzet
Dem hilfft der fromm und lieb Gott.   *Stoll*
Hingegen aber der so sein Vertrauen
Nicht setzen wil in Gottes Macht
Der kan nicht anders als auf Sande bauen
Und wird von jedermann verlacht.   *Stoll*

Abgesang
Dann weilen er hat seinen Gott verlassen
Und seinen Abgott sucht
So bleibt er fort verflucht
Und wil ihn Gott auch hier mit nichten fassen
Ja läst ihn billig sincken
Auch für sich selbst ertrincken:
Darum O Christ
So klug du bist.

In the Prize Song, as it first appears in the opera, Wagner responds to this mixture of masculine and feminine rhymes, but develops his own tauter rhyme scheme as witness of Walther's new mastery. The two *Stollen* build upon Wagenseil's model, with the *Abgesang* more freely composed in a manner that deeply moves Sachs.

Morgenlich leuchtend in rosigem Schein,
Von Blüt und Duft
Geschwellt die Luft,
Von aller Wonnen,
Nie ersonnen,
Ein Garten lud mich ein,
Gast ihm zu sein.

Wonnig entragend dem seligen Raum,
Bot goldner Frucht
Heilsaft'ge Wucht
Mit holden Prangen
Dem Verlangen
An duft'ger Zweige Saum
Herrlich ein Baum.

Sei euch vertraut,
Welch hehres Wunder mir geschehn:
An meiner Seite stand ein Weib,
So hold und schön ich nie gesehn:

Gleich einer Braut
Unfasste sie sanft meinen Leib;
Mit Augen winkend,
Die Hand wies blinkend,
Was ich verlangend begehrt,
Die Frucht so hold und wert
Vom Lebensbaum.

Wagenseil goes on to list various techniques of versifying, such as *Stumpffe Reimen* and *Klingende Reimen* (masculine and feminine rhymes); *Waisen* (orphans), isolated lines with no connecting rhyme, and *Körner* (grains), in which the isolated line connects with a rhyme in another strophe; *Pausen* (pauses), one-syllable words placed at the start or finish, sometimes in the middle, of a strophe (as in the first version of the Prize Song, see Appendix III). David has learnt these and a number of others, as he proudly tells Walther in Act I, scene 2.

However, the main part of the *Tabulatur* consists of the formidable list of thirty-two faults which might be committed, and the penalties they carry. Beckmesser singles out at least seven which he accuses Walther of having committed in his spring song. Rule IV, *Blinde Meinung* (obscure meaning) gives as example 'Ich du sol kommen' for 'Ich und du sollen kommen'. Rule VII, *Laster* (Vice), penalises with two marks so-called 'vicious rhymes', as when in Nuremberg dialect 'Mann' is pronounced 'Mon' to make it rhyme with 'Sohn', or when two or more lines begin with the same word. Rule IX, *Kleb-Sylben* (clipped syllables, or apocope) penalises with half a mark such formulations as 'keim' for 'keinem', and, less understandably, common forms such as 'vom' for 'von dem' or 'zur' for 'zu der'. Rule XI, *Differenz* (difference), deals with misspellings made to give a rhyme, such as 'Deib' for 'Dieb' (one mark), or words unnecessarily repeated to solve a metrical problem, such as 'Der Herr der sprach' (up to three marks). Rule XIII, *Unredbar* (badly constructed) penalises with one mark the arrangement of words differently from that of natural speech. Rule XIV, *Aequivoca* (ambiguity), penalises with four marks the use of two or more words in a verse with the same spelling but different meaning, giving as an example a couplet using the word 'Tocken' ('doll' or 'firing-pin'). *Falsch Gebänd* (false liaison) occurs twice, as Rules XVII and XXIX, and can apply to wrongly connected verses, badly connected *Körner*, or verse and melody being unsynchronised: this carries two or three marks. Beckmesser also refers to 'falsche

Athem', presumably Rule XXI, *Zween Reimen oder Verss in einem Athem* (two rhymes or verses in one breath), carrying a four-mark penalty, when no pause is made where one should be. Beckmesser adds a few more which do not occur in Wagenseil, including *Flickgesang*, 'a song cobbled together', perhaps a resentful dig at Sachs; and two terms, *Schrollen* and *Überfall*, meaningless in the context and evidently brought in to make rhymes with *Stollen* and *allüberall*, thus earning Beckmesser himself categorisation under Rule V, *Blinde Wort* (obscure word).

By some of these strict decrees, Beckmesser can fairly penalise Walther. Rhyming 'Wald' with 'durchhallt' and 'schallt', though later standard German practice, could have lost a mark under rule XXIV, overlooked by Beckmesser, *Lind und hart* (soft and hard). Several times Walther begins successive lines with the same word (*Laster*). Rhyming 'wall't' with 'Allgewalt' is but one example of Walther's *Klebsylben*, his worst fault, and one here making identical sounds rather than rhyme. Some of his locutions could be regarded as *unredbar*, but only by the narrowest interpretation; and there is no reasonable sign of *Aequivoca*, *Falsch Gebänd*, or *Blinde Meinung*. Though to some extent Wagner is playing a private game, the poem has a freedom of expression which tests convention, but a fluency possessing its own logic – exactly calculated to irk the Marker (whether hostile or not) who must go by the book, to confuse the Mastersingers with the unfamiliar, and to seize the imagination of the most sensitive among them. Perhaps Wagner made Sachs the more disposed to be indulgent as Puschmann mentions his regret for his many lapses, caused by neglect of his study in youth.

Wagenseil continues with discussion of the various *Töne* in which verse finds expression. *Ton*, in this context, included in its meaning both the verse and its melody. This was in the proper spirit of Luther, who had written, 'both text and notes, accent, melody and manner of rendering ought to grow out of the true mother tongue and its inflection'. By the verse is here meant the metrical and rhyming scheme of the whole stanza; this might be newly devised, or it might be a successful formula which was taken up and used by later poets, in a manner suggesting a more freely ranging version of the establishment and adoption of variants of the Petrarchan and Elizabethan sonnet. A *Ton* had to consist of at least seven verse lines, but more usually had about twenty; the shortest line could consist of a single syllable (as in Wagner's discarded Dream Song), the longest of thirteen syllables, this being reckoned the most that could be sung in a single breath. Sachs himself is said to have written about 4,300 Mastersongs using 275 *Töne*, of which only thirteen were original. The melody would therefore have to match the number of syllables in each line, though a small amount of decoration would occur (no rhythm was notated, that being dictated by the text); and in transmission it might become varied according to the style of the individual singer and changing musical tastes. Puschmann and Wagenseil both cite one of the most interesting melodies (not least to the Wagnerian), *Der schwartze-Thon Klingsohrs*. In his entry 'Ton' in *The New Grove*, Horst Brunner suggests that this arose around 1235, and quotes four variants between *c*.1340 and *c*.1700. In the thirteenth century it was used for a series of strophic poems belonging to the *Wartburgkrieg*, a source of *Tannhäuser*; at the end of the century the epic *Lohengrin* uses it, as do many fifteenth-century Mastersongs; and between 1537 and 1556 Hans Sachs chose it for no fewer than twenty-two poems.

Nevertheless, new *Töne* were composed, though Wagenseil warns against plagiarism with the injunction that no new melody may repeat as many as four syllables from an earlier *Ton*, and that the shape of the melody and its ornaments must be entirely new. It can then be found sponsors or godparents, will be set to material provided by the Markers, and written down in the *Schulbuch* with the date and the author's name. It will also have to be christened, as in the little ceremony in Wagner's Act III. Some of these baptismal names were descriptive, as with Georg Hagers's 'Extra Short Evening *Ton*' of six lines (one less than the usual bare minimum of seven). Some were impressionistic, like Sachs's own *Morgenweis*, *Guldnerthon*, *Klingender Thon*, and his popular *Silberweis*. Some were of the memorable eccentricity that delighted Wagner when it came to David's recitation; perhaps the most inventive of the Mastersingers in this respect was Ambrosius Metzger, with *Töne* that translate as 'Writing Paper', 'Faithful Pelican', and 'Fat Badger'. And as David ruefully relates to the dismayed Walther, each must be learnt, and sung clearly, in good German, steadily and discreetly with good breath control so as to make clear poetic sense. Every Mastersinger was expected to know the *vier gekrönte Töne*; the first two share an opening phrase distinctive enough to have given Wagner the fanfaring theme associated with the Mastersingers near the start of his Prelude, and that by Heinrich Mügling

(Mögeling) seems to have particularly struck him (see Plate 3.2). Much detail is closely repeated from Wagenseil, who sets out the various grades of student: one not yet familiar with the *Tabulatur* is a *Schüler*, one who knows it a *Schulfreund*, one who can sing five or six *Töne* a *Sänger*, one who writes songs to existing *Töne* a *Dichter*, and one who invents a tone a *Meistersinger*. Beckmesser's

Plate 3.2 The first of the *vier gekrönte Töne*, in Heinrich Mügling's 'long tone', from Johann Christoph Wagenseil's *De Sacri Rom. Imperii libera civitate Norinbergensi commentatio* (Altdorf, 1697).

ultimate failure is thus double. In the *Festwiese*, he cannot properly memorise the words he has taken from Sachs's shop, and turns them into gibberish; furthermore, as he has not heard Walther's melody expressing this poem, he must compose his own, with scarcely less ludicrous results.

It was in Wagenseil's sixth chapter that Wagner found most of the literal detail for the stage circumstances of his first act. A remarkable amount of this survives into the opera. There is the distinction between the *Singschule*, for which the apprentices mistakenly begin erecting the large Markers' *Gemerk*, and the *Frey-Singen* or *Freiung*, in which anyone may take part and at which secular as well as sacred songs were permitted. The singing stool is mentioned, seated on which in the succeeding *Hauptsingen* the singer must await the chief Marker's 'Fanget an!'. Seven mistakes are allowed, and it is insisted that the Marker be impartial on the Marker's behalf (as Beckmesser is reminded by Sachs). Vogel's absence through illness, and the necessary formal apology, are ingeniously used to break the otherwise repetitive roll-call. There are a good many other points of circumstantial detail repeated, though in a number of cases they are altered to suit dramatic convenience: a striking instance is the adjustment of the conditions of *Singschule* and *Freisingen* to make Walther's application and trial immediately acceptable in the strict conventions of the Mastersingers, and the conflation of the three Markers into one to provide Walther with Beckmesser as personal and artistic antagonist.

Wagner, in fact, needs Wagenseil's detail at this early stage of his drama for a complex of reasons. It provides factual circumstance, with an intricacy of reference in a setting that rings vividly true even for audiences with no knowledge of the Mastersingers' authentic practices. There is created an atmosphere of sustaining tradition that is at the same time humorously restrictive; and this is enlivened by Wagner's skilfully affectionate deployment of the detail, coupled with the varying responses to it of David, Walther, Pogner, Beckmesser and Sachs, as well as the corporate confusion of the other Mastersingers. It is by these means that Wagner ensures that it has taken sufficiently deep root in our minds for Sachs's final defence of Mastersong to have authority over Walther's rejection.

4   *Sachs and Schopenhauer*

LUCY BECKETT

All his life Wagner needed the intellectual and imaginative company of creative figures whom he felt to be more or less on his own level. Aeschylus, Shakespeare, Calderón, Goethe and Schiller he read and re-read for decades, his comments on their work often showing a surprising degree of humility and disinterested appreciation in the face of dramatic methods other than his own. Closer to him than any of these, acknowledged by Wagner as a master to be loved and venerated from his first reading of him in 1854 to the touching dream he had about him a week before his own death, was Schopenhauer.

The importance of this one-sided relationship – Schopenhauer failed to respond favourably to the text of *The Ring* and, although he did not die until 1860, never met Wagner – has been widely acknowledged. The exact nature and quality of Schopenhauer's impact on Wagner's works have, however, remained in various respects less than entirely clear. Partly to blame for this has been the almost universal assumption that Schopenhauer's 'influence' on Wagner is most plainly visible in *Tristan* and, to a lesser extent, in *Parsifal*, while the composer's never wholly resolved difficulties with the ending of *Götterdämmerung* are taken to be only the most striking example of Schopenhauer's confirming effect on *The Ring* (of which the libretto had been written before Wagner had heard of *The World as Will and Representation*). There is no doubt that Wagner's reading of Schopenhauer made a considerable difference to the works that, after decades of gestation, emerged as *Götterdämmerung* and *Parsifal*. Nor is there any doubt that *Tristan*, conceived and completed in much less time than any other mature Wagner work, would not have been as it is, and might well not have been at all, if it had not been for Schopenhauer. The connection of Wagner's understanding of the philosopher with the development and

66

eventual exact form of *Die Meistersinger* has, however, been more obscure to observers – partly because of Nietzsche and Thomas Mann, partly because the radiant warmth of the work and its obvious classification as a comedy have made it seem remote from the notorious pessimism and gloom of Schopenhauer, and partly for other reasons peculiar to the character of Sachs.

While owing his philosophy a great deal, Nietzsche reacted strongly against Schopenhauer, and most strongly against the Schopenhauer who recommended both resignation of the will-to-life (or 'renunciation') and sympathy with the suffering of others as the only ethically sound responses to the horrors of the constant conflict of unconscious strivings of which, he had established, life really consists. Nietzsche saw in these recommendations (as did Schopenhauer himself) their consonance with an ancient religious impulse common to Christianity and the East; so did Wagner, who used it most obviously in *Parsifal*, and was savagely condemned by Nietzsche for thus capitulating to 'slave-morality'. In the fragments Nietzsche had assembled for his intended major work *The Will to Power* when his reason finally shattered in 1888, he attacks Schopenhauer for having said that great art both serves and confirms pessimism. 'There is no such thing as pessimistic art', Nietzsche declares. 'Art affirms . . . Art is essentially affirmation, blessing, deification of existence . . . Schopenhauer is wrong when he says that certain works of art [he means Attic tragedy] serve pessimism.' Other fragments assert 'We possess art lest we perish of the truth', and, again in direct refutation of Schopenhauer, that for a tragic poet 'to represent terrible and questionable things' does not teach renunciation but 'shows in itself his instinct for power and magnificence: he does not fear them'.[1]

These remarks, and many others like them, have through a whole century contributed to an almost unexamined consensus that *Tristan*, 'terrible and questionable' as it is, and very far from teaching renunciation, demonstrates both Schopenhauer's shocking conclusions as to the true nature of life, from which we might perish without art, and Wagner's unflinching 'instinct for power and magnificence', his heroic Nietzschean overcoming of ordinary, *ressentiment*-infected humanity. Meanwhile *Die Meistersinger*, affirmative as it plainly is, with Apollo after a successful struggle containing Dionysus in a triumphant assertion of order, must be a Nietzschean rather than a Schopenhauerian work of art. Thomas Mann added powerfully to this consensus, recognising

Schopenhauer's vital contribution to Wagner's life and work but taking a Nietzschean view of it. In one of the key moments in the story of German sensibility, Thomas Buddenbrook, like Mann himself, but also like Wagner, discovers Schopenhauer with deep, thankful delight. Mann, in his marvellous essay of 1933, 'The Sufferings and Greatness of Richard Wagner', quotes the passage in which the hero of his own novel 'experienced the incomparable satisfaction of seeing how a mind of towering superiority seized hold of life – life in all its strength, cruelty and mockery – in order to subdue and condemn it'.[2] Mann goes on to demonstrate the profound connections between Schopenhauer's description of the world and Wagner's liberation into the atmosphere of *Tristan*, connections even more clearly analysed by Mann in his 1935 essay on Schopenhauer. 'Artists often become the traducers of a philosophy, and thus it was that Wagner "understood" Schopenhauer when he placed his erotic mystery play *Tristan und Isolde* under the aegis, so to speak, of Schopenhauer's metaphysic. The part of Schopenhauer's teachings that influenced Wagner, and in which he recognised himself, was the explanation of the world in terms of the "will" or instinctive drive, the erotic conception of the world . . . by which the music of *Tristan* and its cosmogony of longing are shaped . . . Here the erotic sweetness, the intoxicating essence of Schopenhauer's philosophy had been sucked out, so to speak, leaving the wisdom untouched.'[3]

The writings on him of Nietzsche and Mann are the texts most laden with influence in all Wagner criticism. Both of them regard *Tristan* as the most dangerously Schopenhauerian of all works of art, and *Meistersinger* as an obvious exception to the narcotic corruptness of Wagner's music, as 'robustly Lutheran' (Mann), or as a positive summing-up of all that is strongest in German art (Nietzsche). No wonder Schopenhauer's influence on *Tristan* in particular has largely hidden from critical view his simpler, more direct, and healthier (and therefore, both Mann and Nietzsche would have thought, less interesting) effect on *Die Meistersinger*. For what the latter work owes to the philosopher is, quite straightforwardly, its 'wisdom' – something that for reasons of their own both Nietzsche and Mann needed to deny sometimes to Schopenhauer and always to Wagner. Those who agree with Mann – and it takes a steady and unprejudiced historical sense now not to – that Wagner and Nietzsche between them corroded in the sweet intoxicating poison of their combined influence first the moral sense and then the sanity of traditional *bürgerlich* Germany, helping in due course to deliver Nazism to the world, will see not Schopenhauer in *Die Meistersinger* but only a streak of cruelty in the humiliation of Hanslich/Beckmesser, which may be there, and a bullying German imperialism in Sachs's final address, which is certainly not.

In December 1854 Wagner wrote to Liszt about his new discovery. 'Apart from making – slow – progress on my music [Act II of *Die Walküre*] – I have now become exclusively preoccupied with a man who – albeit only in literary form – has entered my lonely life as a gift from heaven. It is Arthur Schopenhauer... His principal idea, the final denial of the will to live, is of terrible seriousness, but it is uniquely redeeming. Of course, it did not strike me as anything new, and nobody can think such a thought if he has not already lived it.'[4] The sense of identity Wagner felt with Schopenhauer, and never thereafter lost, is far from surprising. The man who had already invented the Dutchman, Tannhäuser, Lohengrin and above all Wotan, who felt most keenly the need for release into renunciation from the racking torments of both frustrated desire and frustrated ambition (this was the period in which adequate performance of his works seemed most remote from possibility), was bound to find lasting support and consolation in Schopenhauer's lucid and persuasive exposition of 'the sufferings and greatness' of human life. He was already an inhabitant of the landscape Schopenhauer mapped with the shining conviction of an explorer, and he stayed in it, reassured by the philosopher's analysis of its geography, for the rest of his life.

In an unusually calm, realistic and self-aware letter to his old friend Röckel in 1856, Wagner describes this relationship perfectly. He understands that the optimism of his conscious hopes and ideals had for years been at odds with his 'instinctive and purely objective artistic intuitions', and that the contradiction had been resolved only by Schopenhauer who had 'furnished me with conceptions that are perfectly congruent with my own intuitions'. This 'complete revolution in my rational outlook'[5] which, not being a philosopher, he could never have achieved for himself, has produced the extraordinary gain in personal coherence and clarity that he owes to Schopenhauer. Wagner was right to describe the difference *The World as Will and Representation* had made to him in these definite terms: its effect is readily perceptible in all those works (of which *Tristan* of course is not one) which had already entered the magnetic field of his imagination before his encounter with Schopenhauer and were to be completed after it. It is at its most evident in *Die Meistersinger*.

At the back of his mind in 1854 was the first prose sketch of the work (Text I), written at a single sitting nine years before and waiting for a development it received only in 1861 after the completion of *Tristan*. As in all the slowly-achieved works of Wagner's maturity, the emphasis, the emotional weight of the drama, shifted over time from the young hero conceived by the young Wagner of optimistic idealism (Siegfried, Parsifal, Walther) to the figure of burdened age whose rescue from complicity in the agonising struggle of the phenomenal world – as Schopenhauer had put it – it is for the young hero, whether consciously (Parsifal) or not (Siegfried, Walther), to achieve. Wagner, in other words, having identified with Walther in 1845, became by 1861, and still more later in the 1860s when composing the music, Sachs. The shift would no doubt have taken place – as the shift from Siegfried to Wotan had – without Schopenhauer's map to direct its exact progress; with the map, its course is very clear.

All the important characters and a good deal of the detail, of both action and words, of what was to become the finished work of 1867 are already in place in 1845. Wagner's 'artistic intuitions' have laid out a scenario which needed astonishingly little change to accommodate the Sachs of 1861. There are in the second prose draft (Text II, revised as Text III) a number of small improvements to the mechanics and motivation of the plot, but the single most obvious and most significant change is in the Sachs of the opening of Act III. In 1845 he had, surrounded by large books and neglecting his work, reflected sadly on the decline of German poetry: the weight of this 1845 plot is on the young man (not yet called Walther) and his future as a poet in whose hands Sachs's legacy of inspiration and skill will be safe. In 1861 Sachs is as we know him to be in the finished work, alone at the opening of Act III, 'deeply absorbed in reading a large folio', which turns out to be a history of the world. The draft sketches what will become the *Wahn* monologue in considerable detail, relating, as the libretto will, the folly, delusion and madness evident everywhere in human history to the absurd and dangerous violence of last night's street fight in peaceful, orderly Nuremberg itself, begun by a spark which Sachs already identifies as 'a glow-worm seeking its mate'.

(Interestingly, Wagner has not yet hit on Sachs's specific plan to use the *Wahn* to noble ends.)

Superficially read, this change to what would become ten minutes or so of a long opera might not seem all that momentous: a deepening of the thoughtfulness of a single character who is now moralising about human behaviour in general instead of merely grieving over the fate of an art to which he is famous for having been devoted. In fact this change, particularly if one can absorb it while imagining the music beginning to form in Wagner's mind, colours the whole work. We the audience have moved our position in relation to the events presented on stage. Instead of watching, from safe within a familiar comic convention, the triumph of young love and knightly virtue (Walther as poet, singer and aristocratic but impoverished outsider gaining the hand of the rich man's daughter) and the defeat of a pompous and ludicrously unappealing elderly suitor, we have been shifted to within a central character's sensibility, conscience and responses. This is the position from which audiences are more accustomed to watching tragedy: they see the events of the drama from inside Macbeth, or Hamlet or, eventually, Lear. In spite of the apparent inconsiderableness of what is entirely new in the 1861 prose draft of *Meistersinger*, the whole enterprise, as the finished work which sticks closely to this draft shows, has radically changed in Wagner's imagination. It is now Sachs's point of view, Sachs's feelings and Sachs's consciously-arrived-at moral choice which have become the real focus of the audience's attention, and the prism through which they will see and understand the story and the other characters. Inseparably connected, as the causes of this change, are the emotional storms through which Wagner had come in the 1850s and the book which had explained them to him.

In December 1861, a month after writing the second prose sketch of the work, Wagner wrote to Mathilde Wesendonk from Venice. He had, three years earlier, left her in Zurich with her husband, and briefly and agonisingly met them both in Venice that autumn. 'You'll be wide-eyed with amazement when you see my Mastersingers! Steel yourself against Sachs: you'll fall in love with him! The old sketch had little or nothing to offer. Yes, one needs to have been in Paradise to know what lies hidden here! ... We shall see each other now and then. But without any desire! And thus wholly free! ... Here, in addition, is a Shoemaker's Song! Adieu, my child! – *Der Meister*.'[6] This is a letter not to

Isolde but to Eva – but 'the old sketch' had had, in fact, a great deal to offer.

Wagner fell more deeply in love with Mathilde Wesendonk than with any other woman he had yet come across in a not unchequered emotional career. It is almost certain that the affair was never consummated – that his protestations to this effect, not only to Otto Wesendonk and to the unhappy Minna but also to his sister Clara and others, are to be believed. It is absolutely certain that his passion for Mathilde and what he saw as his noble and selfless renunciation of her to her husband had inspired both *Tristan* and *Die Meistersinger*, and that *The World as Will and Representation* had informed, articulated and crystallised the passion, the renunciation, and in fact both operas. It needs only a little imagination to appreciate the excited sense of vindication with which Wagner must have read Schopenhauer's account of the whole of reality as the blind striving towards life and its generation, with the erotic as its blade, the sharply perceptible edge of struggle in the life of every human being. If this was so – and a wonderfully readable and comprehensible philosopher, with the great Kant behind him, was saying that it was – then Wagner quite understandably felt, first of all, liberated into the possibility of creating an opera that celebrated the erotic as the most real force in human life, even if its ultimate consummation could be discovered only in death. As early as the enthusiastic letter to Liszt of December 1854, Wagner, at the time in the middle of composing the music for the lonely, envious Wotan of Act II of *Die Walküre*, says: 'Since I have never in my life enjoyed the true happiness of love, I intend to erect a further monument to this most beautiful of dreams, a monument in which this love will be properly sated from beginning to end. I have planned in my head a *Tristan und Isolde*, the simplest, but most full-blooded musical conception.'[7] If the jealous nagging of Minna finds its way into Fricka's treatment of Wotan over the love of the Wälsungs in *Die Walküre*, the *Tristan* consummation no doubt records the much-desired, never-achieved resolution of Wagner's feelings for Mathilde; the erotic reality underlying the phenomenal was here put into words, dramatic *representation*, and above all music (for Schopenhauer the highest art) with the philosopher's descriptive sanction and therefore understanding. Or so Wagner obviously felt.

But not with the philosopher's approval. Schopenhauer thought the spectacle he had so brilliantly perceived and described, of the whole of reality as a blind competitive struggle towards life, to be so terrifying and horrible that he was driven to seek out some escape from it for 'the good man'. His carefully-reached ethical conclusions, set out for the human being capable of grasping the true nature of things, are: (a) to renounce the will to life, and particularly the acute pain of the erotic with all the suffering it causes; and (b) to sympathise enough with other sufferers from the misery of being alive to alleviate their pain a little. The renunciation of the first recommendation has nothing to do with suicide, which Schopenhauer takes some trouble to reject as a final *assertion* of the will. Both recommendations are as remote as possible from the erotically-obsessed joint compulsion to the *Liebestod* of *Tristan*, and Wagner understood Schopenhauer quite well enough to realise this.

As he read and re-read the sections of *The World as Will and Representation* which set out Schopenhauer's prescriptions for a good life, Wagner must have been struck, even startled, by the possible ethical depth of the idea he had years earlier sketched for, of all things, a comic opera. It is when Schopenhauer is writing about saints on the one hand and tragedy on the other that he is closest to what Wagner was to make of Sachs. The eventual closeness is beyond coincidence, but coincidence is what must have astonished Wagner at the outset; this no doubt turned to a powerful sense of identity with both Schopenhauer's moral hero and Sachs, as Wagner struggled with his feelings for Mathilde Wesendonk and managed, for once in his life and with the help of considerable fortitude and sense on her part, to behave well.

In sections 68–70 of his book, Schopenhauer describes – not negatively or depressingly, as many would assume he would have done, but with vigour and inspiring, positive warmth – the freeing into the 'love and magnanimity' of renunciation of 'the man entangled in delusion (*Wahn*)'. The contrast pointed here is between 'the hatred and wickedness conditioned by egoism' and the abolition of 'the distinction between our own individuality and that of others' which 'makes possible and explains perfect goodness of disposition, extending to the most disinterested love and the most generous self-sacrifice for others'. In moving from the first to the second, the man who was 'im Wahn befangen' is released into 'what was the enviable life of so many great souls among the Christians, even more among the Hindus and Buddhists, and also among the believers of other religions . . . The inner, direct, and intuitive knowledge from which alone all virtue and holiness can

come is expressed in precisely the same way in the conduct of life.'
'My description', Schopenhauer adds, at the end of a long explanation of this ethical position, 'is only abstract and general, and
therefore cold. As the knowledge from which results the denial of
the will is intuitive and not abstract, it finds its complete expression not in abstract concepts, but only in the deed and in conduct.'[8]

In, Schopenhauer meant, the lives of saints. In, Wagner must
have thought, such noble actions as the renunciation of Mathilde.
In, also, the work of art which has at its centre the good man who
first understands, in 'inner, direct and intuitive knowledge', the
suffering of strife-torn humanity, and then behaves disinterestedly
and generously for the benefit of others.

Schopenhauer's account of such a man, and such a moral
process, matches closely the Sachs it no doubt helped to produce.
'We always picture a very noble character to ourselves as having a
certain trace of silent sadness that is anything but constant
peevishness over daily annoyances... It is a consciousness that
has resulted from knowledge of the vanity of all achievements and
of the suffering of all life, not merely of one's own.'[9] This is in
various ways a peculiarly appropriate comment on the music
which, in the Act III prelude, in the *Wahn* monologue and, most
strikingly of all, in Sachs's reaction to the people's singing of *Wach'
auf!*, conveys his 'silent sadness'. In the emotional decisiveness
with which it is carried out, this compositional feat, like many
others in the work, matches and then much excels in precision the
exalted but untethered view of music as an expressive medium
with which Schopenhauer must have greatly cheered Wagner: 'The
close relation that music has to the true nature of all things can
also explain the fact that, when music suitable to any scene,
action, event or environment is played, it seems to disclose to us
its most secret meaning, and appears to be the most accurate and
distinct commentary on it.'[10] In dealing so effectively with many of
the questions this passage and others like it beg (what kinds of
music? of what quality? in what circumstances?) Wagner was also,
probably quite consciously, meeting another of the philosopher's
definitions: 'Always to see the universal in the particular is
precisely the fundamental characteristic of genius.'[11]

This is, of course, what Sachs himself does in the *Wahn* mono-
logue. With the help of his tome, which cannot fail to suggest *The
World as Will and Representation* on Wagner's lap as he thinks,
Sachs tries to find the cause of the fury and mad suffering men

inflict on each other in the universal *Wahn*. It is the riot of the
previous evening which has made him get out his book. There,
perhaps, he finds a passage such as this: 'In the consciousness that
has reached the highest degree, that is, human consciousness,
egoism . . . must also have reached the highest degree, and the
conflict of individuals conditioned by it must appear in the most
terrible form. Indeed, we see this everywhere before our eyes, in
small things as in great [*Wahn! Wahn! Überall Wahn!*]. At one
time we see it from its dreadful side in the lives of great tyrants
and evildoers, and in world-devastating wars [*In Stadt- und
Weltchronik*]. On another occasion we see its ludicrous side, where
it is the theme of comedy and shows itself particularly in self-
conceit and vanity [*Ein Schuster in seinem Laden/Zieht an des
Wahnes Faden*] . . . We see it in the history of the world and in our
own experience. But it appears most distinctly as soon as any mob
is released from law and order'[12] [*Mann, Weib, Gesell und Kind,/
Fällt sich da an wie toll und blind*]. And so on.

For Sachs to become a complete example of Schopenhauerian
renunciation of the will, of the particular kind of virtue towards
which Wagner saw himself fighting bravely through the Wesendonk
years, he must be afflicted by, and capable of suppressing in
himself, the pain of erotic need (*Not*). The Sachs of the 1845 draft
is not in love with 'the girl' in the scenario: we are still in a conventional comic plot, and her only elderly suitor is the Marker
whom, in the serenade and riot of Act II, Sachs exposes to ridicule
and a good whacking from David simply for the sake of the young
lovers. By 1861 the draft of Act III has enough of the Eva/Sachs
exchange about the badly-fitting shoe to suggest the poignancy of
the eventual scene in the opera, and the first faint suggestion that
Eva feels more for Sachs than the long affection of a neighbour's
child: 'If I did not love the knight so much, I would have chosen
you, if you had won the prize today.' It is tempting to guess that
in the course of writing this draft some notion of the Act II
cobbler's song, which he had sketched by the following month, as
we have seen, occurred to Wagner and suggested Eva's name to
replace the Emma of Acts I and II of this draft. Whether or not
the *Schusterlied*, the bluff, touching lament over the ill-treatment
that angels, as shoemakers, receive from Eve, banished from
Paradise, struck Wagner at this point, it was an inspiration.
It alone (though no musical idea in Wagner ever functions alone)
did a great deal to transform, for the audience, the benevolent

manipulator who was the pre-Schopenhauer Sachs into the noble, self-aware, near-tragic hero, who can identify in himself a possessive desire for his mate and, after conflict both within and outside himself, master his self-will.

These terms, used in connection with a work so celebrated for its sunniness and the happiness of its ending, may seem excessive: if there is a dark streak in *Die Meistersinger* it has usually been found only in the pantomime cruelty of Beckmesser's humiliation. But the terms are Schopenhauer's own. 'Simple, civic tragedy is by no means to be unconditionally rejected', he said in the supplementary chapter (37) to *The World as Will and Representation* called 'On the Aesthetics of Poetry'. Here he describes 'the tragic spirit' like this: 'What gives to everything tragic, whatever the form in which it appears, the characteristic tendency to the sublime, is the dawning of the knowledge that the world and life can afford us no true satisfaction, and are therefore not worth our attachment to them. In this the tragic spirit consists; accordingly it leads to resignation.'[13] This 'Aufgehen der Erkenntniss' is familiar from the philosopher's earlier discussion of 'the changed form of knowledge'[14] from which alone all virtue can come. Here he goes on to make a clear, and no doubt for Wagner thought-provoking, distinction between classical (pagan) tragedy and modern or, as he interestingly calls it, *Christian* tragedy. 'The tragic heroes of the ancients show resolute and stoical subjection under the unavoidable blows of fate; the Christian tragedy, on the other hand, shows the giving up of the whole will-to-live, cheerful abandonment of the world in the consciousness of its worthlessness and vanity.' Hence Shakespeare and Goethe are 'at a higher level' than the Greek tragic poets 'because the ancients had not yet reached the summit and goal of tragedy, or indeed of the view of life generally'. The most remarkable word in this acutely perceptive chapter (which, among other things, cleverly combines Aristotelian 'pity and terror' with Shakespearean 'exalted resignation of the mind in the hero himself') is 'cheerful', *freudiges*. The familiar division between comedy and tragedy here begins to blur – and is further encouraged to do so by Schopenhauer's remarking a little later that comedy itself, in showing 'petty embarrassment, personal fear, momentary anger, secret envy', may convince 'the thoughtful spectator ... that the existence and action of such beings cannot themselves be an end'.[15]

'Cheerful abandonment of the world' in a Christian context as the mark of the tragic hero: this at first sight surprising idea does fit remarkably well the Hamlet of 'There's a special providence in the fall of a sparrow' and the Lear of 'Come, let's away to prison'. It fits no less well the Sachs who recognises that he shares with Beckmesser a middle-aged suitor's selfish, competitive need for the beautiful young girl and overcomes this need in himself even as he defeats the efforts of the absurd Marker. This double 'overcoming' is the real heart of *Die Meistersinger*. More than the flood of feeling, harnessed and ordered in Walther's Prize Song with the help of Sachs's great lesson in the merits of tradition, more than the triumph of young love which the Prize Song finally secures, it moves a responsive audience to a mixture of emotions as hard to define and, particularly, as hard to allocate to either 'comedy' or 'tragedy' as that evoked by Prospero's forgiveness of his enemies, renunciation of his magic power, and resignation of the future to Miranda and Ferdinand.

The detail of its achievement demonstrates a sureness of touch and an economy of means that are the marks, by this time, of Wagner's dramatic genius at its peak. How pleased he must have been to find his 1845 intuitions usable in such a profoundly Schopenhauerian enterprise as the finished work, one can only imagine. Already in 1845 he had planned to match Beckmesser's spiteful marking of Walther's Act I trial song with Sachs's mischievous marking of Beckmesser's serenade in Act II. Only after Schopenhauer (and the renunciation of Mathilde) does Sachs's jealous enjoyment of his destructive marking echo Beckmesser's, and cause Eva to cry out in pain for him as she hears Sachs's cobbling song and realises, for and with the audience, that its grief is for the loss of her. 'O bester Mann!' she sings, through the confusion of Sachs's song, Beckmesser's arrival, Walther's uncomprehending anger, Magdalene's appearance at the window, 'Das ich so Not der machen kann!' Only with Sachs's anguish at the centre of the Act II riot thus firmly fixed in the audience's minds can they pick up the sense of responsibility and remorse from the *Wahn* monologue's memory of the night before when:

Ein Glühwurm fand sein
   Weibchen nicht;
Der hat den Schaden angericht't.
	A glow-worm failed to find
	   its mate;
	It set the trouble off.

In the 1861 draft, and in the longer version of the monologue text which the process of composition enabled Wagner to cut (Texts II and III), the spark of the glow-worm more explicitly lit the raging fire of the street fight. But an attentive audience will not miss the connection between the forlorn glow-worm and the cobbler reflecting on it:

| Ein Schuster in seinem Laden | A cobbler in his shop |
| Zieht an des Wahnes Faden | Plucks at the thread of *Wahn* |

How did he do this? By singing, for example:

| O Eva! Hör' mein' Klageruf | O Eva! hear my lamentation |
| Mein' Not und schwer' Verdrüssen! | My anguish and heavy vexation! |

This infuriated Beckmesser, whose apparent serenading of Magdalene in turn infuriated David, whose rage together with the noise in the street quickly worked up the riot. The use of the David/Magdalene relationship, which in 1845 had been no more than the secondary below-stairs romance of conventional comedy, to fuel the presentation of universal Schopenhauerian strife is wholly characteristic of the work, and of the crucial twist which Wagner's reading of the philosopher gave it. So is the nocturnal degeneration of the orderly craft-guilds of 'mein liebes Nüremberg' into gangs of hooligans clobbering each other in a comic but not unfrightening version of the same self-devouring human conflict. 'Ach, welche Not!', as even Magdalene comments.

In the quiet of the following morning, wonderfully established in the Act III prelude (which music had not yet occurred to Wagner when he wrote the prelude to the whole work) Sachs, having understood the *Wahn* of the night before, and recognised his own part in it, decides to control it – 'ihn bemeistern' – to a noble end – 'ein edler Werk'. The sixteenth-century cobbler, as we have seen, might as well have *The World as Will and Representation* on his lap as a history of the world. Indeed there is only one answer to his question about how to describe *Wahn*: 'Wer gibt den Namen an?' He reaches his *freudiges* abandonment of his own egoistic will as he turns – and the score in the most expansive moment of the whole work turns with him – from night to day, from remembering the raging confusion of *Johannisnacht* to welcoming the radiance, which he will himself achieve, of *Johannistag*.

Only the most superficial acquaintance with Schopenhauer might lead one to deduce from this obvious reversal of the *Tristan* choice of night over day – 'Dem Tage! Dem tückischen Tage . . . dorthin in die Nacht!' – that Wagner had turned his back on the Schopenhauerian perception of the erotic as the deep core of human self-will. On the contrary: Sachs is recognising the truth of this diagnosis with enough clarity and moral strength to deal with his own fierce, grasping motivation and to use, to a good and constructive purpose, the *Wahn* that drives everything. As a poet (composer) the thought is in any case familiar to him. In the scene that follows the *Wahn* monologue he describes the process to Walther (the mature Wagner addressing his younger self), telling him how the Mastersingers made their rules to preserve the power of spring 'in ihren Nöten Wildnis' ('in the desert of our need'). He should know; he is such a master, and the *Wildnis* is where he lives.

He sustains the equanimity of his noble decision until the blissful morning meeting, Prize Song and all, of Walther and Eva in his shop, which is very nearly too much for him. In a storm of feeling which is jealous, self-pitying, anguished, and of course accompanied by the riot music of the night before with his own trouble-inciting cobbling song at its core, he rounds on the happiness of the lovers and evokes from Eva her most impassioned outburst in the whole work. She loves him and always has. This moment, the most piercing in the opera, is certainly the most Schopenhauerian: both words and music invoke *Tristan* as Sachs gives Eva to Walther and finally renounces with 'Herrn Markes Glück' the vortex of the will and the competitive assertion of his own *Not*.

At this last internal crisis in the opera – the 'sweet pain of his heart' is well under control in the quintet, and he does not find it difficult to respond with quiet sadness to 'Wach' auf!' – the triumph of understanding reached in the *Wahn* monologue explains the moral triumph of emotionally costly renunciation. 'Genuine virtue and saintliness of disposition', says Schopenhauer, 'have their first origin not in deliberate free choice (works), but in knowledge (faith), precisely as we developed it also from our principal idea.' If this, coming from an atheist philosopher, has a surprisingly Christian (indeed Augustinian) ring, it is even stranger to find Schopenhauer, shortly afterwards, saying: 'Salvation is to be gained only through faith, in other words, through a changed way of knowledge. This faith can come only through grace and hence as though from without'[16] ('*also wie von Aussen*' – and the words for faith and grace are the ordinary Christian *Glaube* and *Gnade*). In *The World as Will and Representation*? In *Die Meistersinger*, so much affected by it?

What, the reader may well ask, is going on here? Is Sachs after all a chivalrous hero, behaving well in the fashion of a Christian gentleman familiar down the centuries of civilisation – and much scorned by Schopenhauer? Did not Schopenhauer despise *Romantic*, as opposed to *Classical*, poetry for 'maintaining, as effective, motives springing from the Christian myth [and] those of the chivalrous, exaggerated, extravagant, and fantastic principle of honour?'[17] Did he not regard Bellini's *Norma* (of course before Wagner had written anything) as the best example of a modern tragedy precisely because 'no Christians or even Christian sentiments appear in it?'[18]

What we are looking at here is some consequences of the profound inconsistency of Schopenhauer's philosophy, which is, for instance, both explicitly determinist and explicitly demanding of free ethical choice, both explicitly atheist and explicitly sympathetic not just to the sense of aspiration common to all religious expression but to the Christian description of the world as fallen in man and redeemed in Christ. In the great passage (Chapter 70) which forms the conclusion and climax to the original version of *The World as Will and Representation*, Schopenhauer writes again of his 'changed form of knowledge', which alone produces virtuous action, 'that which in the Christian church is very appropriately called *new birth*, and the knowledge from which it springs, *the effect of divine grace*'. This is 'for us the only direct expression of the *freedom of the will* ... The possibility of the freedom that thus manifests itself is man's greatest prerogative ... The animal is without any possibility of freedom ... Therefore the hungry wolf buries its teeth in the flesh of the deer with the same necessity with which the stone falls to the ground, without the possibility of knowledge that it is the mauled as well as the mauler. Necessity is the kingdom of nature; freedom is the kingdom of grace.' ('Notwendigkeit ist das Reich der Natur; Freiheit ist das Reich der Gnade.')[19] It is much more than a coincidence that Sachs, in the *Wahn* monologue freeing himself from his *Not*-haunted world, refers to this very passage as he tries to find its cause.

Warum gar bis aufs Blut	Why, till they draw blood,
Die Leut' sich quälen und schinden	People harass and torment
	one another
In unnütz toller Wut?	In useless, foolish rage?
Hat keiner Lohn	No-one has reward
noch Dank davon;	Or thanks for it;
In Flucht geschlagen	Driven to flight
Wähnt er zu jagen;	He deludes himself he is the
	hunter;
Hört nicht sein eigen	Does not hear his own

Schmerzgekreisch,	Cry of pain,
Wenn er sich wühlt ins eigne Fleisch	When he digs into his own flesh
Wähnt Lust sich zu erzeigen!	He is deluded that he gives
	himself pleasure!

Schopenhauer goes on: 'This self-suppression of the will . . . comes from the innermost relation of knowing and willing in man; hence it comes suddenly as if flying in from without (*wie von Aussen angeflogen*) . . . Behind our existence lies *something else* that becomes accessible to us only by our shaking off the world . . . The doctrine of original sin (affirmation of the will) and of salvation (denial of the will) is really the great truth which constitutes the kernel of Christianity.'[20]

If Schopenhauer actually held that there is a critical distinction between man and the rest of creation, and that 'grace' means something real and has an extra-phenomenal source demanding our free response, he was, some of the time at least, much closer to Christianity than he generally cared to think. He himself would have eluded the charge that he was after all a believer by asserting that the meaning of the life and death of Christ should be taken on a symbolic rather than a literal level. This embarrassment as to what kind of truth is at issue badly confused Wagner's own perception of what was afoot in his works, in *Parsifal* in particular (not to mention the perceptions of many of his critics). The fact that there is no such difficulty with *Die Meistersinger* has caused an altogether different kind of confusion. Because of the period in which it is set and the unproblematically Christian atmosphere of sixteenth-century Nuremberg, the reconnection of Schopenhauer's ethical prescriptions to the solid *bürgerlich* context from which they sprang, but from which they had been separated by the elaborate structure of his whole post-Kantian philosophical system, could take place so easily and naturally that many a connection with Schopenhauer has since been missed.

Wagner himself knew at once that much in Schopenhauer was simply familiar. In the 1854 letter to Liszt he said, still delighted with his new discovery: 'How strange that I have often found your own thoughts here: although you express them differently because you are religious, I nevertheless know that you think exactly the same thing.'[21] Casually delivered in a few phrases in a letter, we here have one of the most significant issues of the last two centuries. Is it possible for truth, somehow or other, to be simultaneously both religious and not? Schopenhauer, the disciplined, careful philosopher, no doubt thought he thought not, whatever the conflicting implications of what he in fact wrote. Wagner, no philosopher but, by instinct and training, as much an old-German perfectionist master craftsman of ancient Christian tradition as Schopenhauer (or Sachs, or Thomas Mann who recognised the affinity), thought that the spiritual/secular line was a blurred affair which by the middle of the nineteenth century, whose sophisticated liberal lateness had not escaped him, no longer needed definition. Nietzsche, clearer-headed than Wagner and less ambivalent about him and much else than Mann was, built on the atheism in Schopenhauer and dispensed altogether with both the ethics and the sympathy with religious aspiration. Either Nietzsche or Mann might have seen in the character of Sachs wonderfully convincing proof that Schopenhauer had left behind less than he asserted of the long Christian past of his culture and his country – but this was not what either of them was looking for in *Die Meistersinger*. Meanwhile the very various discoveries of Darwin, Freud, Einstein and their successors have continued to confirm how far and in how many respects Schopenhauer's entirely philosophical view of reality was ahead of its time; and his moral insight, which so productively and positively informs *Die Meistersinger*, has largely been lost from view. It was, and is, in a period obsessed with progress, new neither then nor now.

Schopenhauer's ethical conclusions have probably reached more people through this one opera than by any other channel. But if audiences thought, and think, that what they have seen and heard is not much to do with philosophy and a great deal to do with 'ordinary' goodness and truth, they will have been quite right. Schopenhauer's 'influence' on Wagner is mostly a question of the composer (not being, as he once remarked, 'lucky' enough to be, like Liszt, 'religious') looking, as many who live in the ruins of Christian civilisation look, for confirmation of what he already felt to be the case, and alighting with joy on a formidably argued and intellectually more than respectable presentation of it. Then he did what he could with what he had discovered, and the result was one of the greatest of all masterpieces.

5 Richard Wagner and Hans Sachs

MICHAEL TANNER

One of the most captivating features of *Die Meistersinger*, as one gets to know it ever better, is the labyrinthine nature of the work, rather like the Nuremberg that used to be depicted in Act II. Enticing alleys may lead nowhere; but, unlike the lovers, one does not want to escape but to get to its centre, supposing that it has one. As with the lovers, one finds that Hans Sachs casts his light and shadow everywhere over the proceedings, providing links that may turn out to be distractions, both with his creator and with every other character and theme of the complex drama. Musically things are otherwise: the overture, for example, makes no specific reference to him. David tells Walther that he is the pupil of 'der grösste Meister', and names him, but we hear no more of him until the Masters enter in Scene 2, and then he sidles in inconspicuously. During the remainder of Act I he is established as a man of reason and moderation, though his proposal that the prize the next day should go to the people's favourite is radical. And of course he is more sympathetic to Walther than anyone else is, and the curtain on the act memorably comes down with him alone on the stage, wondering. But musically speaking he makes a muted impression: one remembers what he said rather than how he said it. All the other main figures of the drama are more vividly characterised than he is by this point, even Magdalene.

Yet the terms in which one finally thinks about *Die Meistersinger* are almost entirely set by Sachs, whose concepts and plans come to dominate the drama, and our grasp of it, ever more completely, and whose name is the last word we hear from the jubilant crowd, sweeping aside even thoughts of 'heil'ge deutsche Kunst'. It is almost as if Wagner, most uncharacteristically, is finding out what the subject-matter of his work is as he goes along, and that may be the reason why many people find Act I diffuse and comparatively lacking in interest. It can seem like a prolonged exposition which actually is not so much concerned with the central issues of the drama as the time it takes would indicate. Wagner can even give the impression that he is employing a set of delaying tactics which make one impatient for him to get to what really matters.

The overture itself is unique in his output for being relatively unrelated to what will be the central themes of the drama. But not only – it goes without saying – could one not bear to be without it, but it is also, for us, inconceivable that the work should begin in any other way. Significantly, and unusually, Wagner wrote it first, when he still had some work to do on the details of the action. In being so entirely festive, and at the same time so 'learned', it puts one into a frame of mind which is gradually, so to speak, withdrawn by the drama until it is reasserted, by monumental recapitulation, in the final scene of Act III. People who argue, and many have, that the drama is completed with the Quintet, and that the last scene is a too-obvious working out of what we know must occur, might as well claim that the overture is a mistake too, though of a different kind. Both might be alleged to be irrelevant to almost everything that occurs between them. All Wagner's preludes command attention, if only, as in Siegfried, by leading us to wonder what on earth is going on. But the overture to Die Meistersinger is his most grandiloquent as well as his most grand gesture, inviting our complicity in a world of self-assured values at the same time as leading us to a slight querying of whether so overpoweringly robust an assertion could ever be wholly justified. And, notoriously, it draws attention to its own virtuosity: the indispensable triangle stroke that heralds the contrapuntal handling of the three main subjects is a kind of arrow pointing us to what Wagner can do. The manner in which the overture relates most closely to the rest of the work is its simultaneous concern with establishing a general attitude towards life and its celebration of the art of music itself, and the impeccable craftsmanship of this musician who had so often been impeached.

It is this incessant intertwining, or indistinguishableness, of means and ends, subjects and treatments, form and content, which induces a Rausch which is both typically Wagnerian but quite unique to this work. Wagner appears both to be telling us that we have never heard anything like this before, and also drawing on the accumulated resources of two centuries of consummate music-making – Nietzsche calls it 'magnificent, overcharged, heavy, late art' in his celebrated critique of it in *Beyond Good and Evil*. If we feel less inclined than he did to search out dangerous symptoms in it, we are lured by Wagner into a glowing acceptance that the world which contains *this* must be a fundamentally sound one: it presents itself to us as a kind of secular theodicy. What it does not do, and what Wagner's overtures are usually remarkable for doing, is to create in us a sense of urgent issues to be announced and resolved. The only prelude comparable to it in this respect is that to *Lohengrin*, which gives us a static vision of beatitude, complete in itself, and gives Wagner a problem that he fails to solve: how to get the drama under way without a drastic lowering of temperature. No doubt it taught him a lesson, since he never made the mistake again, and in *Die Meistersinger* he achieves instead the first of the many staggering *coups de théâtre* that the work contains by not bringing the overture to a close, but hurling us straight into the congregation's chorale.

And, having allowed himself an overture without even premonitions of conflict, he gets to work with extreme speed when the curtain goes up, juxtaposing the lines of the hymn with the amorous cooings of various solo instruments, as Walther and Eva make eyes at one another. At the same time he performs the first of several similar tricks by having the congregation sing words which, it will turn out much later, are deeply relevant to the relationship between Sachs and Walther. They are singing the praises of John the Baptist, whose feast day falls on the morrow, and so we pay no particular attention. But the chorale melody will return at a crucial stage in Act III, just before the Quintet, and the bearing of the words on the action will become retrospectively apparent during the opening parts of that act.

What Wagner does in the overture, and continues to do in Act I, is to give us a world which is so familiar and secure that we take it to be the everyday one, in all its heterogeneity and range of feeling, even though the mood of the overture is to so large an extent unified. The feeling of the chorale, which is certainly not inferior to anything in the great tradition of German sacred music, is something that we observe rather than participate in, partly because of the way it emerges from the overture, partly because of the carryings-on between lines. It serves to reaffirm, from a different perspective from that of the overture, the beauty in the ordinariness of the everyday life that we are confident we are going to see depicted. Wagner, the great intellectual among composers, at least until Schoenberg, who nonetheless produces music of constant and unsurpassed sensuousness, the dramatist who only seems concerned with extreme states of consciousness, ecstasy being achieved after appallingly prolonged agony, here goes to the limit in reassuring us that he too is at home in the areas where most of us spend our lives. Passion, such as the enormous orchestral climax, with the organ weighing in, as the congregation leaves the church, subsides quickly and provides only momentary excitement. And so Act I continues, offering us a fairly comprehensive conspectus of the quotidian, accompanied by unflagging ingenuity in the orchestra. Take any ten minutes of the act, and you will be unable to deny the wit, resource and humanity of what you hear (and preferably see). But people get restive: is there a subject-matter here, sufficient to sustain the evident scale of the work, or is it Arnold Bennett set to music?

The answer, as so often with Wagner, is to wait and see. From the vantage-point of the end of the work, there is nothing in Act I that is irrelevant or redundant. Once more the self-referential quality of *Die Meistersinger* is apparent. Wagner, here a cobbler-poet, has a handful of threads which will be carefully interwoven as the action proceeds. That is not to say that many of the incidental delights are only justified by their place in the whole. For instance, David's lengthy recitation of the modes and tones has as its primary dramatic point the nature of teaching, which in his case is very bad teaching. He is the kind of instructor that every student dreads, concerned far more with impressing his captive audience with the extent of his knowledge than conveying any idea of the principles by which it is organised, or finding out whether they are following what he is saying. And, since the material of his exposition is creation, it is not surprising that Walther's reaction is one of bemused revulsion, bumptious and arrogant as he himself is. We are confronted with the worst kind of teacher addressing the most reluctant kind of learner: David is a potential successor to Beckmesser (so perhaps Beckmesser was once a David), while Walther is, or could become, one of those people whose sole criterion for art is spontaneity. That is the comedy of their non-communication. Wagner himself is present throughout the scene in the ingenuity with which he makes pedantry delightful, and petulance tolerable. And so, even at this rudimentary stage of the action, we are vouchsafed an underlying wisdom, a perspective which is typical of comedy, leaving us in no doubt that things will turn out well, though Wagner is keeping us in the dark as to how that could happen. For unhelpful as David's methods are, he is telling the truth; and sympathetic – up to a point – as Walther's reactions are, he is complacently ignorant. The kind of fanatical identification with his characters which is Wagner's hallmark in most of his work is notably absent here, and will remain so until Sachs takes over command in Act II.

At any rate, the amused presentation of David and Walther does give us a genuine issue, though the Apprentices' merrymaking at its failure to get anywhere concludes the scene appropriately, and leads with natural ease into the entry of the Masters. Musically speaking, Wagner's 'art of transition' is nowhere more strikingly manifest than in *Die Meistersinger*, where changes of mood are at least as abrupt as in his other works, but musically just as expertly managed. We move from the tenor-orientated teaching scene to a predominance of self-consciously solemn basses and baritones. The rapidity with which the characters of Pogner and Beckmesser are established, the contrast between secure, well-padded benevolence and jumpy, tense anxiety is remarkable; while Walther's eagerness, also not untinged by nerves, is expressed in flowing musical phrases which fit only awkwardly what he has to say, conveying the embarrassment he feels at the lie he is telling Pogner, that 'though I forgot to mention it yesterday, it was to be a Mastersinger' that he came to Nuremberg. Fortunately two further Masters arrive for Pogner to greet, and Walther has a chance to muster his courage and say, once more over-floridly, that he hopes to win the prize. All this is on top of, rather than accompanied by, a rich orchestral fabric leading to the moment when Kothner calls the roll. As one after another of the Masters answers his name – not forgetting the Shakespearean touch when Niklaus Vogel's apprentice explains that he is absent through illness, and the Masters wish him good health – the dense contrapuntal texture continues on its sumptuous way, and again it is clear that Wagner is not only revelling in his virtuosity but also stressing to us that we are in the presence of individuals whom he wants us to see as bathed in his affection. It is an extraordinarily moving episode, and yet it would be possible to feel that Wagner is primarily concerned to display to us his big-heartedness. He and Sachs, it seems, have indistinguishable views of life, but at this stage Sachs is only one, so far not significant, character among others, so what Wagner later embodies in him is something that at this stage he has to do for himself.

When in Act III Sachs rebukes Walther for disparaging the Masters, he says 'You are dealing with men of honour, who make mistakes and are content to be taken on their own terms.' But Wagner has already been telling us this as they enter and the roll is called. The point about the Masters is important enough to be made twice, especially in the light of the reception of Walther's Trial Song, but is the parade of all-comprehending humaneness not a bit too emphatic, so that Sachs himself can be seen as rather preening, and his creator like George Eliot at her most strenuously benign?

One would have to answer these questions affirmatively, and feel that one should be given the chance to make up one's own mind about the Masters, and about the general distribution of sympathy among the characters, or perhaps feel that the issue was unresolvable, were Wagner not operating at a level that renders them irrelevant. Or rather, that is the level that he eventually operates on. His methods here are not as distinct as one might expect from those of *Tristan und Isolde*, with which *Die Meistersinger* is routinely contrasted in a comprehensive way. In both, Wagner is operating with a metaphysic – in large part the same one, an idiosyncratic interpretation of Schopenhauer. But in both works he approaches the metaphysic in easy stages. For in Act I of *Tristan*, we are living in a world of extremely intense emotion, in which both the lovers-to-be stress how much they are not saying, though we are aware of what this is. But what, in the duet in Act II, and crucially in the invitation that Tristan extends to Isolde to follow him to the 'Wunderreich der Nacht' after King Mark's lament, and still more during his second prolonged monologue in Act III, they express is a set of views that must surprise them as much as it does us, as they move from depth to depth of insight into the nature of the world which their passion demands if it is to be fulfilled. The big difference from *Die Meistersinger* is that the prelude to *Tristan* has already alerted us to the imminence of something remote from our normal experience, while the overture to *Die Meistersinger* leaves us wholly unprepared. Sachs makes, so far as we can tell, no discoveries during the course of the opera. His wisdom, as most explicitly stated in the *Wahn* monologue in Act III, and put into brilliant practice in the scenes that follow, is long-pondered. It is in the course of Act III that experience – in the form of understanding the unprecedented violence of the previous evening, and coping with an unruly young pop-star – puts it to a test that it triumphantly passes. But the recessive Sachs of Act I has not yet had an opportunity to expound his views, and in any case it is part of his outlook that he should mix with his social group without trying to convert them to a *Weltanschauung* which they would not understand, or would not believe if they could understand it.

Wagner's task is more difficult. As soon as Sachs has the opportunity to give vent to his attitudes and emotions, we no longer feel that there is authorial intrusion, since Wagner has a spokesman. But until then he has to indicate that there is more to the events taking place on the stage than there appears to be. He does, among other things, set himself the absurdly difficult task in Act I of setting an absolutely typical committee meeting to music. His own disposition was as admirably unsuited to his being a good committee-man as one can imagine. The patience required to deal with windbags, self-promoters apparently speaking from firmly-held principles, inarticulate people with excellent points to make but lacking the persuasive power to make them effectively, head-strong characters who want to cut through all the crap – that was not in his repertoire, except for the last category. All the more remarkable is his capacity to give an artistic rendering of just such a set of people in fruitless debate. The only indulgence he allows himself, and one that is fully justified in dramatic terms, is that it should all break up in acrimonious turmoil. Until then, and up to Walther's abortive Trial song, and between its verses, Wagner has provided an unceasingly witty commentary on the proceedings, some of it mock-solemn, as in the bass cluckings of the Mastersingers' theme after Nachtigall's puzzled 'Merkwürd'ger Fall!' and the brief fugal passage beginning at Beckmesser's 'Sagt, konnt ein Sinn unsinniger sein?'

The 'authorial presence' is not, of course, original to Wagner among opera composers; nearly every one has employed it, but none is so insistent as Wagner, and none provides us with so little choice about how we should respond. In this respect *Die Meister-singer* is the most, not the least, typical of his works. An exceptionally blatant example occurs later, when the song contest is taking place. While poor Beckmesser has only his own mistuned lute to accompany him in his attempt at the Prize Song, Walther is awarded the full supportive and approving orchestral works. Is it good enough to say that this is a comedy, and that in comedies the dramatist has a licence to be unfair, since he is only imitating life? Or, more specifically, that it incites us to cruel laughter, and that laughter is at least as often derisive as it is expressive of fellow-feeling? Probably it *is* good enough, but the interesting thing about *Die Meistersinger* is that it is the most serious of comedies in that it forces us to ask those questions. It has, after all, at its centre a uniquely powerfully expressed bleakness, and has presented us with one incident that offers corroboration of that view. Sachs's *Wahn* monologue is, for most of its length, a poignant reflection on the folly of human existence; and the riot of the previous evening, in an adequate performance, comes across as something really savage and disturbing. Wagner's amused account, in *Mein Leben*, of the origins of that scene in his own early experience of a milder episode of the same kind, should not mislead us into underestimating the transformation that he effected. In general, the study of the sources, in his life and in the early drafts, of any of Wagner's works should always be conducted with the thought in mind that what counts is what he actually produced, which may well be something very remote from what he began with. Trite as I hope this observation is, the obsession of many Wagner scholars with the evolution of his works does often lead them to the conclusion that what he ended up producing was really an inflation of something which was, in the first place, less pregnant or pretentious. And in the case of *Die Meistersinger* in particular, one is doing less than justice to it if one is not prepared to entertain the possibility of a fairly drastic critique of it as a whole, even if the critique can be satisfactorily answered.

By identifying with Sachs to the extent that he does, Wagner is both playing God and suggesting that it is all right to do that, but also, in the crowd's veneration of Sachs, postulating a sense of rightness in ordinary people which it is a fundamental tenet of Sachs's outlook to deny. Again, that could be said to be a basic constituent of 'the comic vision'. Comedy arises from the follies and accidents which are inseparable from being human, but suggests that somehow they will work out for the best. But what, it seems, Wagner is attempting in *Die Meistersinger* is a unique contribution to the genre, or a new genre, so far lacking successors: noble comedy. Moments of nobility are not uncommon in comedy, and may indeed be necessary to bring it to a happy resolution; but to build a whole massive work round one may be thought excessive, and in a way that one would expect from this composer. In all his works but least appropriately in this one, he makes peculiarly acute the feeling that he is contriving – and in some ways with astonishing success, thanks to his overpowering genius as musical rhetorician – to have the best of all worlds, helping himself to whatever takes his wide-ranging fancy, but a fancy that always seems to be dignifying itself as the last word. And that sets up an opposition which is perhaps as deep as anything else in anti-Wagnerians. Could there not be an element of the tentative, a willingness to concede that 'other modes of existence are possible'? Even Sachs's whimsical acknowledgment of his inability to answer the question 'Wer weiss, wie das geschah?' ('Who knows how that came about?') at the climax of the *Wahn* monologue seems to carry with it the implication that if he doesn't have an answer, then there isn't one to be found. He embraces the comic vision, and Wagner assists him by his massive modulation from the E major of Johannisnacht into the C major of Johannistag – an anti-*Tristan* assertion of the value of day over night.

But the crucial point is that when night gives way to day, it is not a matter of reality taking over from illusion, as it is for the lovers in *Tristan* when day gives way to night. If we take the *Wahn* monologue to be, in its pivotal place in the dramatic structure, a compressed counterpart of the duet in Act II of *Tristan*, two salient things come into focus. First, and this might seem comically banal, there is the sheer fact that it is a monologue and not a duet, which, however, has the most profound implications for the nature of *Die Meistersinger*'s vision of the world. Second, in the progression of thought and feeling that the monologue presents in so compact a way, there is no question of an insight into reality replacing a complacent acceptance of appearance. Sachs, and with him Wagner, have arrived at the last stage of Nietzsche's six-part history of western thought as he hilariously presents it in *Twilight of the Idols* (German title: *Götzendämmerung*): 'The true world we have abolished. What world has remained? The apparent one perhaps? But no! *With the true world we have also abolished the apparent one*' (Nietzsche's italics). A little less succinctly: the history of western thought has been dominated by the opposition between appearance and reality. Since, as Nietzsche tirelessly and rightly insists, the fundamental motivation of philosophers has been moral, their metaphysics called into being to justify their moral cravings, then if one abolishes the metaphysics, the morality which it allegedly underpinned is deprived of its support. Once the opposition between the apparent (everyday) world and the true (metaphysical) world is eradicated, the 'apparent' becomes the 'true'. Traditional metaphysics, on this diagnosis (to which much of Nietzsche's work is devoted), is the expression of discontent with the life we are familiar with, and no-one would have been more appalled than Nietzsche if we did not suffer from that discontent – no-one, that is, except Wagner. But it is a discontent which can only be profitably employed by being understood, not by being assuaged or gratified by something which answers to its needs.

In religious terms, it is redemption that people chronically seek – redemption from their fallen state, or less self-censoriously, from the wretchedly inadequate conditions of life. What for the Christian is gained by repentant submission to the will of God is adumbrated, at least, by the metaphysician as knowledge of the true world. But if the 'true world' is banished, then what are we to do about those urgent, unresting feelings that many of us suffer, for a state in which we are freed from the miseries, self-generated or externally inflicted, of existence? Any answer will sound very unglamorous compared to the emotional and spiritual pyrotechnics of religion and transcendent metaphysics. We have to find some way of *coping* – a word that irresistibly suggests harassed housewives with far too much to do in the kitchen before the children get home. But it is possible to cope in other ways than grimly getting on with the chores, or putting up with frustrations. As the Marschallin, a sub-Sachs figure, says in her monologue in Act I of *Der Rosenkavalier,* 'Und in dem "Wie" da liegt der ganze Unterschied' ('And in the "how" – there lies the whole difference'). Nietzsche saw, roughly speaking, two alternatives: the advent of nihilism, in which we cease to apply value to anything whatever, or the advent of the *Übermensch,* the self-creating and thus value-creating being, about whom he remained notoriously vague. Wagner spent his life envisaging alternative solutions, several of them apparently espousing metaphysical systems introduced at the imperious behest of his protagonists' needs, of which *Tristan* is the most extreme example.

At a celebrated and crucial moment in *Die Meistersinger* Wagner quotes the most famous motif from *Tristan,* while Sachs tells Eva that he is clever and, knowing the 'sad tale' of Tristan and Isolde, is not prepared to undergo King Mark's fate. But he is saying, or implying, vastly more than that: he is emphatically *not* saying that Eva and Walther can become Isolde and Tristan, and that he will not be the cuckold. Eva, in her huge outburst 'O Sachs! Mein Freund!' that precedes his disclaimer, is clearly shaping up for the role of Isolde, being passionately heartfelt and yet letting herself go, dramatising her feelings to the limit. In his reply Sachs cuts her off, and Wagner stems the flow of Tristanesque music by reminding us of the insidious power of the genuine article. In the whole context, the *Sehnsucht*-motif almost induces revulsion: 'Not that, for heaven's sake!' It is not just the role of King Mark that Sachs is rejecting, but the whole ethos in which it is possible to be King Mark, as the music indicates by brusquely and boisterously reasserting the *Meistersinger* world, so that Eva's brief flirtation with the metaphysics of transcendent love is conclusively scotched, and the next time she opens her mouth it is to sing the opening phrases of the Quintet, ecstatic but firmly rooted in the emotional realities of the situation. Isolde could never sing that music, any more than Eva could ever launch into the *Liebestod* (to give it its wrong name). The Quintet, that deliberately too-short moment of stasis, is the point at which they all have their feelings clear, and are able to give uninhibited expression to them, because there is no call for reticence, except on Sachs's part, and he is well-covered by the other four. Only his melodic line, not what he is saying, registers.

The Quintet is another of the moments in which *Die Meistersinger* conveys to us forcefully the glory of art, at the same time as it marks the private resolution of the crises that the characters have been living through. All that is needed now is the integration of these lives into the society which has so far not accommodated Walther and Eva, and thus not let Sachs have his way. In seeming to break his own rules, as laid down above all in *Opera and Drama*, Wagner is surely showing us that even when the prescriptions for an art come from the highest source – its greatest practitioners – they still have to be tested, just as Sachs had insisted in Act I that the people should check the Mastersingers' rules annually to ensure that they do not ossify. For the point of all rules that are worth keeping is the end they serve, and Wagner's dramatic ends are here fulfilled by something that he had *a priori* proscribed. But when he repeatedly stressed the absurdity of ensemble-singing, in criticism of previous opera, he had clearly not envisaged a dramatic situation in which the only way to convey its essence was indeed to have an ensemble – and because it is unique, the extraordinary nature of the harmoniousness that it celebrates is highlighted. If, as is often claimed, Wagner identified with both Walther and Sachs (a false claim, I think), here, at any rate, in letting his inspiration flood forth, while producing something that is 'technically' irreproachable, he has produced his own Prize Ensemble, and his most hostile critics are subdued by its glory.

Sachs leads up to the launching of the Quintet by singing in a robustly traditional way, and using the chorale melody which opened the opera proper as his basis, with virile enhancement from the orchestra. His identification with the John the Baptist about whom the congregation sang at the start is clear: they used the tune to celebrate the forerunner of the Saviour. But now the terms of the drama have become wholly artistic – religion makes its appearance in the work only to quit the scene immediately – so Sachs is the Baptist who prepares the way for the birth of the child (the Prize Song) who will save, artistically, the human situation, so that Walther will be acclaimed as the prize-winner. Sachs is aware of the role he is assuming, and he had, in the closing passage of the *Wahn* monologue, stated that this was what he was going to be and do. The way in which he has organised things is as practical, and untranscendental, as can be imagined. He has set things up for a couple who are unusual only in that the man is a most gifted composer and performer, and has ensured that they will be 'as happy as men understand happiness', to use the slightly cutting words of the Marschallin at the end of the Trio; though Sachs has none of her animus towards the young pair. Perhaps because he does not overestimate the happiness of married life, Sachs finds it easier to let Eva go. 'I once had a wife, and children enough', he tells Eva in their dialogue in Act II, without notable regret (and with no further elucidation). And the musings of the *Wahn* monologue are not those of a man who believes that there is a validity to passion which will enable anyone to escape the omnipresent manifestations of illusion. Enthusiastic abandonment of one's individuality is not, in *Die Meistersinger*, a way to salvation, for two reasons: first, because it is not an achievable condition; second, because the whole notion of 'redemption' which Wagner so ruthlessly explored and exploited throughout his works is here discounted, and it is this rather than anything else that gives *Die Meistersinger* its uniqueness in his *oeuvre*.

In *The Case of Wagner*, Section 3, Nietzsche writes sarcastically (for once giving his acumen a rest) 'there is nothing that Wagner has pondered more deeply than the problem of redemption. Who if not Wagner would teach us . . . that beautiful maidens most like to be seduced by a knight who is a Wagnerian? (the case in *Die Meistersinger*).' But Walther is by no means a redeemer, and he is not the child that Sachs is Baptist to. It is surely, among other things, because of the absence of aspirations to redemption that *Die Meistersinger* is a work that non-Wagnerians do not feel makes unwholesome demands on them. Wagner is not less concerned here than in his other works with our relationship to the world, but he reaches widely acceptable conclusions on the basis of premises which are darkly pessimistic. I have found that calling *Die Meistersinger* a pessimistic work tends to engender either incredulity or scorn. But that is the result of taking the overture as the microcosm of the whole work. The prelude to Act III and the *Wahn* monologue are clearly its most deeply-felt passages, and undeniably pessimistic in tone. And the opening theme of the Act III prelude, first heard as a counterpoint to the third verse of Sachs's Cobbler's Song in Act II, when Eva says 'The song pains me, I don't know why', punctuates Act III, never letting us forget the pervasiveness of *Wahn*. Sachs, like Schopenhauer and unlike almost all philosophers in the western tradition, does find value in the world, but it is negative. That, it can be argued – Nietzsche argued it – is better than finding no value in the world at all. I think that Nietzsche was right, and that the most terrifying view of the world is one in which we can find no value of any kind in it. Finding negative value – 'Wahn, Wahn, überall Wahn!' – at least means that we have something to judge by. Life has meaning, even if it is of the wrong sort. And if *Wahn* is, though ubiquitous, still capable of being manipulated for nobler ends, as Sachs ends his monologue by saying, then that is still better. But the optimism is clearly tenuous, the idea of progress absurd, the threat of imminent catastrophe always something to be faced.

Basing a decision as to whether a work is optimistic or pessimistic, on whether it is a comedy or a tragedy or, crudely, on how many corpses there are around at the end, is hopelessly simple-minded. The great comedies characteristically leave one with a more uncomfortable mixture of feelings than the great tragedies. How does one feel at the end of *Così fan tutte*? And notoriously at the end of *Le nozze di Figaro*, Mozart's least perplexing great opera, one reflects that the sublimity of the Countess's forgiveness will soon be in demand again, once the Count has recovered from his spasm of shame. On the opposite side, at the end of *Tristan*, however deluded the lovers may be in their ideal of a transcendence of their selves, they certainly die believing that that is what they are about to achieve, and so are, in Tristan's case, deliriously happy, and in Isolde's radiantly transfigured (Wagner thought of her in terms of Titian's *Assumption*, one of the supreme masterpieces of levitating ecstasy).

Comedy is rarely cosy, and in any case cosiness is rather depressing. No doubt the jubilations of Johannistag deserve all the C major that Wagner can award them, but which key will the next day be in, when the burghers get back to work, Sachs continues his depressing studies of *Stadt- und Weltchronik*, and Eva and Walther begin looking for a house to settle down in? Wagner rather diverts attention from these questions by leaving us with Sachs's final address, which may not be the miscalculation that it is often taken for, but does raise new, far from encouraging, issues.

That aside, though, *Die Meistersinger* is a profoundly troubled work, because the forces that Wagner can find it in himself honestly to present as bulwarks against encroaching destructive *Wahn* are, within the drama, highly contingent and not very durable – the cries of 'heil'ge deutsche Kunst' are optimistic in the critical sense. That, no doubt, is why the *Wahn* motif occurs so frequently, and in some strange-seeming places: after Walther has sung the *Abgesang* of the first verse of the Prize Song to Sachs; more intensely (*molto ritenuto* and *sehr ausdrucksvoll*) after the second verse; during the orchestral pantomime accompanying Beckmesser's wanderings round Sachs's workroom, just before he discovers the text of the Song; with tremendous force – its only fortissimo rendering – after Walther has sung the third verse to Eva; at length after the 'Wach' auf!' chorus, and as Sachs begins his address to the crowd; and for the last time as the crowd celebrates Walther's triumphant performance. Even if one extends one's view of it from being expressive of Sachs's resignation (or renunciation) to his being deeply moved in general, its expressive burden is just that – a burden. The fact that Sachs responds over and over again to the Prize Song with pain suggests that he finds in it, for all his admiration, something of a promise which he knows cannot be fulfilled. And in its violence after the third verse sung in his workshop there is even anger – it will do the trick, indeed has already done it so far as Eva is concerned, but it won't last. Perhaps that is connected with its content, and the unreflective way in which everyone else adores it: no doubt it will be at the top of the charts, but for how long? It is Walther's ever-increasing ardour, as he moves from singing about a lovely garden to having a woman beside him, and the combination in his dream of Parnassus and Paradise – art and life united – that enthuses everyone else, but stirs the sadness in Sachs. The Prize Song, like its singer, is glamorous and full of youthful visions. But that is because, as Sachs explains to Walther, 'spring sang for [him]'. A true Master is one who can go on singing beautiful songs during the less thrilling stretches of life – and who can guarantee to be able to do that? Sachs says hopefully that the Masters' rules will be an indispensable help, but admits that re-capturing, or retaining, the vision of spring is something one does 'so gut er kann'. And Walther's character, as we are led to perceive it, does not seem too promising, while Sachs himself has abandoned mastersinging.

It is an achievement of *Die Meistersinger* that one's focus on it keeps on moving from the outside – consideration of the whole monumental work – to areas within it, and that this process never stops. The work itself seems to defy the gloom of its hero's outlook, while concentrating our minds wonderfully on what precisely that is, and why we should accept it. We make a mistake if we try to decide which, finally, of those, and other possible perspectives, is the right one. But Wagner has ensured that we shall not be able to rest from the attempt, and that is one reason why we feel about it, as Sachs feels about the Trial song in his *Flieder* monologue, that 'it sounds so old, and yet is so new'.

6 'Die Meistersinger': naive or sentimental art?

LUCY BECKETT

More than any other work for the operatic stage, *Die Meistersinger* is about the medium in which it is written. In words and music, in verse and melody, in *song*, it describes, analyses, criticises and presents *song*, verse and melody, words and music. The sophistication of this enterprise is what drew from Nietzsche his deeply ambivalent tribute to the work in *Beyond Good and Evil*.

It is a piece of magnificent, gorgeous, heavy, latter-day art, which has the pride to presuppose two centuries of music as still living, in order that it may be understood ... It impresses us at one time as ancient, at another time as foreign, bitter, and too modern, it is as arbitrary as it is pompously traditional, it is not infrequently roguish, still oftener rough and coarse ... [It] includes *especially* the joy of the artist in himself, which he refuses to conceal, his astonished, happy cognisance of his mastery of the expedients here employed, the new, newly acquired, imperfectly tested expedients of art which he seems to betray to us.[1]

Coloured though this description is by the clashing admiration and contempt with which by this time (1886) Nietzsche regarded Wagner and all his works, it gives an accurate impression of some of the particular qualities of the opera which distinguish it both from the other music dramas of Wagner's maturity and from the works of other operatic composers.

A century later, two separate passages from Carl Dahlhaus's essays on Wagner, expanded from his contribution to *The New Grove*, underpin Nietzsche's impression with an interesting choice of generic terms. The first passage, from an essay on Wagner's aesthetics, concerns the presence of Wagner in all his music dramas 'in defiance of the maxim that the dramatist must be invisible behind the events he depicts'. 'In the music dramas', Dahlhaus writes,

Wagner is an epic writer: he does not allow the *dramatis personae* to become independent, but continually interrupts them with his own comments and asides ... The choice of subject, the musical technique, and the Romantic principle of expression act together to create, not a thoroughly 'objectivized' action at one remove from the dramatist, but a musical epic, in which the narrator, commenting on the events and reflecting the emotions, is really the principal character.[2]

The second passage is from Dahlhaus's account of *Die Meistersinger* itself in his essay on Wagner's works:

The impression that diatonicism has been reinvested with its old, 'classical' rights is completely illusory: what is denied is always present, even though unexpressed. Chromaticism has become the normal language of music, the rule to which diatonicism is now the exception, conspicuous because unusual . . . The diatonicism of *Die Meistersinger* is somehow dreamlike, not quite real in the 1860s; the style of the work is less a restoration than a reconstruction, it is 'secondary' diatonicism, in the sense of Hegel's 'secondary' nature.[3]

The lateness of *Die Meistersinger* in relation to the history and language of western music, the composer's presence as 'the principal character' in the drama and his 'joy in himself' and in his 'mastery', the application of the Aristotelian distinction between 'epic' and 'dramatic' and of the Hegelian term 'secondary' to its musical style: these are useful pointers in the direction of a description of the work that might begin to do something like justice to its unique quality. But they need to be deployed and combined with great caution, and with close reference to the detail of the work. At first sight, one might think, for example, that however appropriate the 'epic' label might be to *The Ring* or *Parsifal*, *Die Meistersinger*, with its unity of time, action and place, its array of realistically drawn characters, and, above all, its central figure through whose sensibility the events of the story are seen, judged and ordered, must deserve to be called, with full conviction, a 'drama'. Surely the characters and plot do have a sufficiently independent, 'objectivised', life of their own to form (as do Shakespeare's characters and plots) an opaque screen between audience and dramatist? Even if, as we must, we answer this question in the affirmative, Dahlhaus's 'musical epic', partly in combination with the 'secondary' qualification he gives the diatonicism of the work, is helpful as a lens through which to look at the oddness of *Die Meistersinger*.

C. S. Lewis put the phrase 'secondary epic' into critical currency when he used it to describe the difference between Homer, and other 'primary' epics with a long oral pre-history, on the one hand, and Virgil and Milton on the other. Homer never intervenes 'with his own comments and asides'; it is not a sense of the poet

that we derive from the *Iliad* and the *Odyssey* but a sense of his
heroes and their fates. From the *Aeneid* and *Paradise Lost*, by
contrast, we cannot fail to assemble a powerful, complex impression of Virgil and Milton. Virgil's own perception of the sadness
and transience of things, of the equivocal triumphs of conquest and
empire, reach us through the irony, self-doubt and torn conscience
of Aeneas. Milton's personal fight with his rational mind to establish for himself the justice of 'the ways of God to men' reaches us
through his own sympathy for Satan as well as for Adam; for the
spirit of enmity to God as well as for the victim of the impulse to
disobey. Both the *Aeneid* and *Paradise Lost*, in other words, strike
us as 'modern', self-conscious, *'sentimentalisch'* in Schiller's definition, reflective and reflexive works, through which we are brought
sharply up against the complex imagination and painfully arrived-
at judgement of an individual, who sat alone at his desk and wrote
himself into his characters and plot. The same is evidently true of
all Wagner's works, but of *Die Meistersinger* with particular clarity
because of the quick susceptibility and ordering consciousness of
Sachs at its centre and heart. Sachs, like Aeneas, is the hero who
both suffers and succeeds, and whose mixed view of the other
characters we are made to share, and we feel with him and for
him so acutely because of his creator's self-identification with him.

   Perhaps surprisingly, a momentary comparison of *Die
Meistersinger* with *Paradise Lost* is even more instructive. For
Paradise Lost, also, is about the medium in which it is written.
The poem is an argument conducted, through the story of Adam
and Eve, between Milton and a God who may or may not be
good, may or may not be going to prevail, in the end, over evil. If
the argument concludes in an agreement that the dealings of God
with the human race are just, then the reader may be convinced
that this has been shown to be the case. The medium of the poem
is persuasive language, particularly rhetorical speech: the whole is
intended to persuade, and each part is also intended to persuade –
someone, another character, the character who is speaking, the
poet himself, the reader. This is as true of the descriptive passages
as it is of the many different kinds of speech in the poem, and,
throughout, the quality of the rhetoric, its honesty, weight, logic,
bias, are analysed and measured by the critical poet even as it is
delivered. The parallel with *Die Meistersinger* is obvious: the medium
of the opera is music, particularly song: the whole is intended
to order feeling (love, jealousy, courage, conflict, unanimity) and

to delight, with harmony, discord, convention and breaking of convention, appropriate and inappropriate matching of melody to verse; and so is each part. This is as true of the descriptive and conversational passages as it is of the many different kinds of song in the opera, and, throughout, the quality of the score (words and music in combination), its emotional truthfulness and weight, its inventiveness and lyrical inspiration, are analysed and measured by the critical writer/composer even as it is delivered. One result, for the audience or reader, is that sense of security, of being in the hands of an artist who knows exactly what he is doing over the whole extent of a long work, that only the greatest masterpieces give.

One of the things that Wagner does in *Die Meistersinger*, as in no other of his music-dramas, is to play – play with the audience, and with his own, by this time virtuoso, skill as writer and composer. Nietzsche was right to draw attention to the 'joy' of the work, wrong to go on to complain that it has 'no beauty, no South . . . nothing of grace, no dance'. Nietzsche, by the 1880s, would allow nothing German (except his own mind and prose) to have any lightness of touch, any clarity or any speed. Elsewhere in *Beyond Good and Evil* he contrasts the heaviness of everything German with 'the South', represented by Machiavelli and Petronius.

How could the German language imitate the *tempo* of Machiavelli who . . . cannot help presenting the most serious events in a boisterous *allegrissimo*, perhaps not without a malicious artistic sense of the contrast he ventures to present – long, heavy, difficult, dangerous thoughts, and a *tempo* of the gallop, and of the best, most cheerful humour? Who would venture on a German translation of Petronius who . . . was a master of *presto* in invention, ideas, and words? What matter in the end about the swamps of the sick, evil world . . . when like him, one has the feet of a wind . . . which makes everything healthy, by making everything *run*?[4]

These remarks have a bearing on *Die Meistersinger* which Nietzsche would certainly have denied, though his own acknowledgment of Wagner's 'happy cognisance' in this work 'of his mastery of the expedients here employed' suggests the speed and confidence, and the playfulness, which characterise so much of the work.

As obvious example is the pantomime music for Beckmesser when he limps into Sachs's workshop in Act III and finds the words of Walther's first attempt at the prize song written down by Sachs. Stáge directions, description of how he feels now, his memories of the night before: all are given to the audience by the orchestra. So is his glimpse of the song, in a snatch of the melody that we have heard but he has not – and which he will be quite unable to find when Sachs has given him the words to make a fool of himself with. It is swiftly done, a piece of connivance between Wagner and the audience which is over in a few seconds. The moment, later in the scene, when Sachs commits Eva to Walther, thus avoiding for himself King Mark's fate, is full of pathos and point but is achieved, to the words 'Mein Kind/von Tristan und Isolde/kenn' ich ein traurig Stück', with a musical reference to Wagner's latest work. The reference, remote, to say the least, from the cultural equipment of a sixteenth-century cobbler, is there for the audience to catch across the briefly recognised gap, of willingly suspended disbelief, that separates them from what is going on on stage, which is, among other things, a *play*.

Shakespeare quite often takes hands, as it were, with his audience across this gap. When Prospero has dismissed the spirit-actors of his 'insubstantial pageant', his wistful glance at the passing fragility of even 'the great globe itself' gives the audience a moment's complicity in Shakespeare's sadness at his departure from the London theatre. When, in the Forest of Arden, Orlando interrupts a sharp, oblique prose conversation between Jaques and Rosalind with the limp line 'Good day and happiness, dear Rosalind', and Jaques stumps off with the crisp farewell 'Nay then, God be with you, if you talk in blank verse', the audience remembers with amusement that Jaques's own great speech on human folly was in blank verse – and began 'All the world's a stage'. *As You Like It* is, as it happens, yet another text that is at least partly about the medium in which it is written: the shifting relationships between love, truth and melancholy, verse, prose and song, natural and artificial arrangements of words, beset the play. Orlando, who posts feeble poems on trees and goes about talking to himself in truncated sonnets, learns about love from the forth-rightness of Rosalind's prose, but when Rosalind's intelligence and good sense have sorted four lovers into the right two pairs, the language of the play is resolved into a formal quartet of bemused assent that is as far from an imitation of the way in which people really talk as the *Die Meistersinger* quintet, or as Jaques's farewell, in blank verse and finally even in couplets, at the end of the play.

The songs in *As You Like It* are of winter and spring, hunting and love; the poetry in the rest of the text is of age and youth, solitude and company, hunting for a mate, forgiveness and love. Some of the writing is bad and evidently placed as bad; some of it is merely presented to the audience without qualification or criticism as the medium in which the characters are truly themselves, and some of this is prose rather than verse. Only Duke Senior and Jaques deliver, to an on-stage audience as well as to the audience in the theatre, formal statements in measured verse of themselves and their own philosophies. In *Die Meistersinger*, where the medium of thought and felt life is a combination of words and music, all these elements, from actual song to mere conversation, are present, as are other Shakespearean devices, notably the soliloquy, not used in *As You Like It*; but the range, scale and complexity of their deployment are very much greater.

After the prelude, song, as itself, begins the work, the lines of the congregation's chorale producing at once a sense of community and harmony, as hymns are designed to do, but interspersed with the music of *Not*, of, so far light, sexual feeling and intrigue, which soon becomes the emotional undercurrent across which Walther and Eva, Magdalene and David throw the conversational exchanges of the first scene. This ends, setting a precedent which will be followed later in the work, but which is far removed from Wagner's declared operatic theory (and practice in the *Ring* and *Tristan*), with a flight of feeling from Walther at 'Neu ist mein Herz' and a miniature trio in which the voices of Eva and Magdalene join his to conclude the scene on a C major chord and the rhyme 'Mut/Hut/gut'. There has not yet been enough actual song in the work for the audience to sense that what they are hearing here occupies what can best be described as the middle ground, the area of musical and verbal form, that is, which lies between actual song on the one hand and conversation or soliloquy, reciative with various kinds of accompaniment, on the other. Not all that much of the whole work takes place on this middle ground, but some of its best moments do.

The rest of the first act establishes how much singing goes on in sixteenth-century Nuremberg, how highly its formal correctness is valued, how necessary the acquisition of its techniques is for entry into the *bürgerlich* charmed circle of skill and prosperity that runs the city (and has the beautiful, marriageable daughters), and how long it takes a humble apprentice – in song as well as in his everyday craft – to become a Master. The apprentices sing as they rearrange the church as a song school; David, on the verge of becoming a journeyman, demonstrates, to Walther's horrified amazement, how much he has already learnt of the complicated

rules of Mastersinging; and the Masters themselves give convincing
proof of their proficiency in the art. Only some of the time, however, does Wagner convey all this to the audience in singing which
clearly represents actual song. David's long list of the 'tones'
which the apprentice must memorise accurately, and Kothner's
quotation from the *Tabulatur* – arranged in neat four-line stanzas of couplets with a six-liner to round it off and a flourish of
Koloratur at each full stop, all framed in lines of (sung) speech for
contrast – both illustrate plainly what the Masters are supposed to
be able to do. In the middle ground, however, of words and music
representing not song itself but formal speech or heightened feeling
or both, are Kothner's roll call of the assembled masters, Pogner's
elaborate address announcing that Eva is to be the prize at the
singing competition on the next day, and the angry, but still tidy,
contrasting chunks of verse with which Sachs and Beckmesser defy
each other just before the song school collapses into furious noise.

All this sets out with formidable impressiveness what Walther,
an impoverished knight from the Franconian countryside who has
learnt how to sing from one old book and the beauty of the
natural world, is up against. But this is a comedy, and something
of a fairy story, as well as a nostalgic presentation of a safe moral
world in which art and honour and goodness are to be perceived
as connected, as they were certainly not in the second half of the
nineteenth century; so Walther must deserve, and be able to earn,
Eva just as surely as Ferdinand (for example) deserves and is able
to earn Miranda, or Orlando Rosalind.

Only once in the first act does Walther sing an actual song, his
official trial song, scornfully scratched by Beckmesser's jealous
marking into the highly-charged confusion in which the song
school breaks up. But Walther's formal account of himself to the
Masters, which they hear not as a song but as an instinctively
composed poem, gives the audience a clearer sense than his trial
song does of his promise as a potential Mastersinger. 'Am stillen
Herd' has two carefully matched opening stanzas – 'Zwei art'ge
Stollen', Vogelgesang calls them – with the word 'Vogelweid'
identically placed, and a deft third section, so that its structure is
that of an AAB *Bar* mastersong. It belongs, nevertheless, to the
middle ground, of speech heightened by music but not meant to
be perceived as song, and it is Walther's most impressive moment
before his morning dream of Act III. It is the strong emotional
pulse of his trial song itself that will haunt Sachs in the second act,

but his singing of it has to compete not only with Beckmesser's spite but with the angry altercation of the Mastersingers and the gleeful mockery of the apprentices' repeat of the ironic quatrain with which David wished Walther well. In the skilfully suggested noise in which the song founders, Wagner is sustaining three different kinds of music simultaneously, and in only one of them, the Mastersingers' argument, is music not representing music.

By the end of Act I Wagner has established a continuum of musical and verbal expression that goes all the way from actual singing to the recitative, with varying orchestral accompaniment, commentary and gloss (in both senses), which is, at differing degrees of intensity, the 'ordinary' language of his music dramas. At the extremes of this continuum music is used on the one hand to represent itself, and on the other to represent the currents of feeling, reference, memory that underlie conversation or reflection either in the minds of the character or in the minds of the audience directed by the composer (or, of course, both). In what we have called the middle ground are patches of the score in which elements from both ends of the continuum – formal melody and end-rhymed stanzas from the one, flexibility of emotional expression from the other – combine to produce what audiences have always felt to be the moments particularly characteristic of this work. These moments are more like the high points of other composers' operas than anything else in mature Wagner, yet, para-doxically, they are given their particular quality by the extremes of the continuum that support and frame them. Of this quality 'Am stillen Herd' is the clearest example in Act I.

The second act opens with the extremes: with the apprentices singing a song as they shut up shop, and resuming it (with some sharp new words: 'Der Alte freit/die junge Maid/der Bursche die alte Jungfer!') after a passage of recitative conversation between David and Magdalene. Pogner's little scene with Eva begins with him reflecting, in relaxed recitative, and ends, similarly, with the con-versations between him and Eva and between Eva and Magdalene. But at its centre there is a moment of lyrical expansion when he tells his daughter, in both comparatively formal verse and com-paratively organised melody, of the festival to come and the part she will have to play in awarding the prize, which is herself, before 'die ganze Stadt'. As in the gradual arrival of the Mastersingers in Act I, as in Sachs's four lines of verse celebrating 'mein liebes Nüremberg' in the middle of the *Wahn* monologue, the music here

collects itself in tribute to the city-as-community, which functions
in this opera as a reality even more than as an idea.

The score returns briefly to recitative as Sachs packs David
off home and then opens into one of its supreme middle-ground
moments as Sachs, alone under the elder-tree, muses on Walther's
trial song. It is because of all that he has laid down in Act I that
Wagner can here give us, by combining Sachs's recitative vocal
line with the not-quite-clear reminiscence of Walther's melody and
its given harmony, a wonderful impression of someone silently
remembering actual music. At 'Dem Vogel, der heut' sang', Sachs,
as if coming to a conclusion about Walther's singing which is his
own and will be resolutely held, and almost as if now speaking out
loud after quiet thought, delivers the last quatrain of his monologue to a firm, new and moving melodic line.

The conversation between Sachs and Eva, full of dramatic
subtlety and darkened towards its end by Sachs's unhappiness as
he discovers the strength of Eva's feeling for Walther, is conducted
in lyrical recitative, the audience gathering its changing emotional
colour from both the vocal line and the orchestra, as light, probing
words are exchanged between two people who have known each
other a long time and are not sure of the feeling there is or might
be between them. When Walther appears he tells Eva angrily of
his humiliating experience in the song school: the contrast with the
Flieder monologue could not be more vivid, although the same
scene is being recalled, as Walther's rapid, outraged couplets, clearly
speech rather than song of any kind, are rattled through with an
effect that takes the score into yet another area of convention and
expression. With the silence of the evening re-established by the
Nightwatchman's actual song as he tells the hour, Wagner embarks
on the scene in which music as music, music as feeling and
anguished speech, music as noise, and (eventually) music as
silence, combine to enthral, amuse, shock and touch the audience
in a way that demonstrates exactly what Nietzsche meant by 'the
joy of the artist in himself'. Sachs's rousing, pained cobbler's song,
designed to infuriate Beckmesser and grieve the Eva he has lost to
Walther, Beckmesser's wonky serenade 'marked' by Sachs's
hammerblows delivered with relish and only twice on the first beat
of any bar, the miraculously audible exchanges between Walther
and Eva, showing that they know each other so little that he has
no idea why she is upset, and the riot – violent disorder in peaceful
Nuremberg – that swamps the stage in confused sound: all fade

quickly to silence as the Nightwatchman returns to the suddenly empty street. It is an extraordinary operatic *tour de force.*

The silence with which the third act begins is quite different, not the silence of the absence of noise but the silence of thought, filled, not this time with music, but with melancholy and the effort to understand. The prelude gives the audience this atmosphere, and what they see, as the curtain rises, attaches it clearly to Sachs's early-morning study of a large book. The opening scene of the act is written so that David's comings and goings, and even his apprentice song, to a formal little chorale tune (after a false start to Beckmesser's serenade), make no impression on it: Wagner is again sustaining several kinds of musical language simultaneously, but in a way that is particular to this short scene. The music of Sachs's brooding flowers into the *Wahn* monologue, an obvious middle-ground passage of great significance to the whole work but, in its unity of intention, a less remarkable compositional idea than the *Flieder* monologue. Walther's singing lesson, however, has Wagner using his whole continuum once more, and in a way that curiously parallels the course of the Act I song school, though the outcome is so much happier. There is some preliminary recitative conversation, lit by the wonder of Walther's dream. Then Walther asks Sachs a simple question, 'Ein schönes Lied, ein Meisterlied:/wie fass' ich da den Unterschied?', much as Kothner asked him who his master was in Act I. Sachs's reply, like 'Am stillen Herd', is a beautiful poem in *Bar* form (here AABB), with 'Jugendzeit' and 'Winterzeit' in identical positions as the repeated 'Vogelweid' was, and punctuated by remarks in tidy couplets from Walther. 'Mein Freund! In holder Jugendzeit' is no more intended to be heard by the audience as a formal song than 'Am stillen Herd' was: for contrast, as with Walther's trial song in Act I, we shortly hear his first attempt at the Prize Song, with Sachs's friendly and precise comments between its stanzas. But just as 'Am stillen Herd' convinced us of Walther's quality as a potential Mastersinger, so 'Mein Freund! In holder Jugendzeit' convinces us of Sachs's already-achieved skill – and contributes much to our sense that this scene is a lesson in respect, truthfulness, patience and courage as well as in singing. That its melody returns briefly in the orchestra as Sachs, after organising Beckmesser's come-uppance, sees Eva approaching, only adds a little of his private pain to this sense.

For the emotional climax of the work, Sachs's stricken but resolute consigning of Eva to Walther, Wagner has everything he needs to hand: the concluding section of the prize song for Walther to dazzle Eva with, the increasingly bitter recitative, almost turning into the song of the night before, in which Sachs laments the fate of the rejected cobbler, the quotation from *Tristan* after Eva's outburst of feeling, and the Baptist's chorale from the opening of the work to which Sachs sets up the formal christening of the new *Meisterlied*. But then Wagner adds something entirely new, new to this work, new to music drama, and against all its principles: the quintet. Here the dazed happiness of the two pairs of lovers, which has been delivered and blessed by Sachs (who has given David as well as Walther his status and his bride), and his own pride in the victory over himself that he has achieved through his seeing of Walther's song into the world, are expressed in words and music which give the audience an unforgettable impression of the kind of harmony which in real life is wordless and soundless.

At the *Festwiese* we are back with a great deal of music as music: noise, first of all, but cheerful noise now, as fanfares sound and converging marches sort themselves out; then the singing of each guild as it arrives, and a clumping dance, really danced by apprentices and their girls; then more fanfares and the Mastersingers' own march; and then – public and general harmony, as the quintet was private and personal harmony – the whole city's singing of the 'Wach auf' chorale, the historical Sachs's own words used as a tribute, in music, to this character in an opera. This gives Wagner his opportunity for the most powerful contrast, within the spectrum of musical language he has established, in the entire work: the silence of Sachs, in the brooding music of the Act III prelude and the *Wahn* monologue, as he is too moved to speak. When he does respond, he speaks, and Pogner replies, in the first recitative passage in the scene, and we return to the middle ground of formal verse and sustained and concluded melody, that is nevertheless not music representing music. After two more actual songs, Beckmesser's hopeless attempt at Walther's poem, muddling the sense of the words like Peter Quince and caught fast in his doomed serenade tune, and Walther's triumphant improvement on his initial effort in the workshop, Sachs takes command of the shocked silence that greets Walther's refusal to accept membership of the Mastersingers' guild, and his final speech, in words that the rest of the work has surely justified, celebrates the goodness and truth of art, in music taken up and sung by the assembled people of his city. Elements of epic, elements of tragedy, elements, even, of pastoral escape into a prelapsarian world where the natural and the creative are at one – 'Dem Vogel, der heut' sang/dem war der Schnabel hold gewachsen' – are all present in the work. But this is a true comedy ending, in which the restoration of order to a community disrupted by *Wahn*, and the right disentanglement of romantic muddle for married happiness, have been satisfyingly achieved and sealed, sending the audience out of the theatre warmed and encouraged, as do *The Marriage of Figaro*, *As You Like It*, and all the other great comedies.

A little earlier in his account of *Die Meistersinger* already referred to, Dahlhaus uses Schiller's distinction between 'naive' and 'sentimental' art to define the musical lateness and self-consciousness of the opera that, after all, immediately followed *Tristan*: 'The "old German" simplicity of *Die Meistersinger*, represented by diatonicism, is by no means "naive" but "sentimental": not instinctive but relative and nostalgic.'[5] This is of course the case. One only has to compare for a moment the whole musical enterprise of *Die Meistersinger* with Verdi's *Don Carlos*, an exactly contemporary piece, also set in the mid sixteenth century, to recognise the appropriateness of Dahlhaus's use of the Schiller distinction: Verdi's is the 'naive' opera, even though his text is derived from the 'sentimental' Schiller play. And yet one cannot help suggesting, in any attempt to describe exactly what it is that makes *Meistersinger* different from Wagner's other music dramas and, for all the ironic reflexiveness of its musical language, different from any other post-Romantic work for the stage, that the resolution of conflict it presents takes place in a 'naive' context of conviction and assumption impervious to irony and the destructive impulse of the *Not*-tormented soul.

The key to this puzzle is that art, both the subject and the achievement of the work, both its medium and at first sight the substance of its message, actually works throughout the opera as a metaphor. Walther does not deserve Eva as his bride until he has shown that his passion and youthful instinct for freedom can be ordered and disciplined within the rules of the society of which she is the carefully nurtured (by Sachs as well as by Pogner) pride and prize. In pointed contrast, Beckmesser's expertise in these rules cannot produce from him the living feeling which inspires generous and truthful action. Sachs's renunciation of Eva to Walther, of which his selfless assistance at the birth of Walther's song is both means and image, demonstrates his mastery over himself and his own feelings through the metaphor of his mastery of the rules of art. Even Pogner's fairytale insistence that Eva must choose a Mastersinger for bridegroom or remain unmarried, even David's promotion to journeyman which fits him for marriage, have their place in this metaphorical structure. In the end the restraint, balance, sanity, harmony and health of art properly achieved *represent*, in the work, the restraint, balance, sanity, harmony and health of real human goodness, tempered by discipline to deal with the chances and changes of a whole lifetime, in Sachs's words:

viel Not und Sorg' im Leben;	much need and hardship in life;
manch' ehlich Glück daneben;	much married happiness as well;
Kindtauf', Geschäfte, Zweit	baptism, business, disputes
und Streit.	and quarrels.

This triumph of Apollo over Dionysus does not cancel the presence of Dionysus, any more than the triumph of the diatonic cancels the presence of the chromatic in the score. But it is not the morally neutral triumph of Nietzschean will to power. By whatever complicated Schopenhauerian route Wagner himself had been led to his own delivery of this work, its declaration that real goodness, real beauty, real truth exist and are guaranteed by what unites them and is outside any work of art, stands, making this both a sentimental *and* a naive *Meisterlied*, an 'ewiges Werk' unclouded by the equivocal judgement that always shadows Wotan's.

7 'Wahn', words and music

> The theme of the third act on which I am now working
> is: *Wahn! Wahn! Überall Wahn!*; this theme is brought
> out everywhere ... it is the theme which rules my own
> life and the lives of all noble hearts; would we have to
> struggle, suffer and make sacrifices if the world were
> not ruled by *Wahn* ? ... If Hans Sachs did not know a
> way of using *Wahn* to some nobler end, and if his
> Walther had not beckoned to him from the royal castle
> at Nuremberg, oh how sad would my theme sound
> today! But the music I hear is *Wach' auf, es nahet gen
> den Tag.*
>
> Wagner to King Ludwig, 22 November 1866

At the creative centre of *Die Meistersinger*, and crucially placed
some two-thirds of the way through the work, lies the *Wahn* monologue. The word *Wahn* itself must stay in German, for there is no
English equivalent. Indeed, it is of the essence of German that
many abstract nouns have an area of meaning, filled with resonances, rather than the closer definitions that characterise most
other European languages. 'Illusion' is generally felt to be the nearest
equivalent of this much-debated, essentially Schopenhauerian word,
in the sense that it can represent the false illusion that leads men
astray as well as the ennobling illusion presented in art, destructive
disorder as well as healing artistic order. Wagner's opera drama-
tises the tension between order and disorder, and further, between
balance and constriction (as opposing attributes of order), and
between adventure and chaos (as opposing attributes of disorder).
Since this is also a work of art taking art as its central metaphor,
the relationship between verbal and musical expression of these
ideas is exceptionally close, even for Wagner. The nature of the
Wahn monologue exemplifies this.

A comparison of the second draft libretto, Text V, with the
final version in the score (see Appendix I) will suggest how
Wagner's mind acted musically on the formation of his poetry so
as to express his ideas. The first thirty-six lines of the soliloquy,
down to 'fängt der da an zu rasen!', are virtually the same in both
versions. It may be noted only that in the first draft libretto, Text
IV (which has no significant differences from Text V), Wagner
added in the margin as an afterthought the important lines 'in

111

Flucht geschlagen/meint er zu jagen', which he amended from
'meint' to 'wähnt' in the score: the meaning is much the same, but
the resonance clearly different. However, from 'Mann, Weib, Gesell
und Kind' to the end there are elaborate changes. The dropping of
the lines elaborating the glow-worm image (and a couple of others)
improved the emphasis, but the reordering of the remainder gave
Wagner a better logical sequence of ideas that guided, or more
likely was guided by, his sense of musical structure.

He opens the soliloquy, then, in the D major of the previous
scene with the cello and bass melody associated, from Sachs's
cobbling song in Act II, with his brooding over the world's *Wahn*
(Ex. 7.24). This comes to rest on a low F sharp, over which the
bass trombone introduces Sachs's cry of 'Wahn!' on a C natural.
C is the fundamental key in the opera of order, stability and reason;
but here it is made into the discordant tritone (an opposition to F
sharp that has been growing in force throughout the opera), and
Wagner promptly abandons a key signature for an indeterminate
A minor. The following passage is declaimed in a hesitant
recitative accompanied at first by no more than stray phrases and
chords. The climax on a dominant seventh on A does not return
to the key of D: after a bar's pause the music settles on C (a dominant pedal in the new key of F), at 'Wie friedsam treuer Sitten', for
Sachs's contemplation of his beloved Nuremberg (Ex. 7.18: an idea
Wagner may have remembered from Meyerbeer's *Les Huguenots*
in the so-called 'Bénédiction des poignards'). But this is soon
tonally destroyed with reminiscences of the riot's horror. Sachs
lands on octave As at the end of his phrase, 'zieht an des Wahnes
Faden', and the music continues for these reminiscences on an A
seeming to function as a dominant pedal preparing the ground for
a return to the D of the monologue's opening and the 'Wahn' key
area. But the expected return to D, further suggested by the bass
line at 'Prügel regnen, mit Hieben, Stoss' und Dreschen den
Wuthesbrand' is overshot at 'zu löschen', to land on D sharp as
the bass note of a diminished seventh F sharp–A–C–D sharp (=E
flat): Sachs then outlines this himself with 'Gott weiss, wie das
geschah?' from C down to F sharp. Another pause of nearly a
bar, and (using themes from the midsummer spell and the riot of
Act II: Exx. 7.10 and 7.19) Wagner begins the real recovery of
musical order with Sachs's growing understanding and with it
his resolve. 'Ein Kobold half wohl da: ein Glühwurm fand sein
Weibchen nicht' begins in B major, the key of the midsummer

spell, but with a dominant ninth on F sharp (Sachs's last note, F sharp, is also his first note in the new harmonic context). 'Der hat den Schaden angericht't' drops the key a minor third from B to G sharp (written for convenience as A flat). 'Der Flieder war's: – Johannisnacht!' drops another third to E major; and with the move from night to day, from nocturnal chaos to the hope of light and order, 'Nun aber kam Johannistag!', there is a rapturous turn to the festival theme (Ex. 7.20) with the final drop of a third taking the music home to C for the rest of the soliloquy. It is achieved in no more than three pages of score with a swiftly dropping chain of thirds. The themes articulate what is being said; but it is Wagner's tonal strategy, available to him once he has got the poetry ordered, that presents the struggle and Sachs's decision to turn the bad *Wahn* to the good, cost him what it may.

   Since the opera so much concerns the creation or recovery of order from disarray, and since the central metaphor is art and specifically the marrying of poetry to music, Wagner needs to express this with all his own art, at every level. Walther's three songs exemplify his achieving of this artistic marriage in his relationship to the *Bar* form of the Masters he seeks to join.[1] The first, 'Am stillen Herd', is a narration rather than a song: there is no suggestion that Walther is actually singing here. When Kothner asks with whom he studied, he answers, from reading a great master, Walther von der Vogelweide, and listening to the forest birds (Wagner is of course emphasising genius released by private study and natural inspiration, not formal instruction: his own story, as he saw it). Walther's instinct is such that after his first two paragraphs Kunz Vogelgesang (impressed, sneers Beckmesser, with all this stuff about birds, *Vögel*) points out that he has made two skilful *Stollen*. The fact that his *Stollen* consist (as heard by us) of seventeen bars and not a regular sixteen bars (as heard by the Mastersingers) is accounted for by his pause in each before going on to his second line, allowing Wagner to insert in the orchestra for the first his wintry low E, and for the second his vernal arpeggio. Walther's verses have made a point about the contrast between confining winter and releasing spring. However, his *Abgesang* bears too little relation to his two *Stollen* for it to be a satisfactory completion, both in the poetry and especially in the musical irregularity with which Wagner confirms it. In answer to Beckmesser's triumphant demand to know if anyone can make sense of this torrent of words, even the two 'bird' Mastersingers, Vogelgesang and

Nachtigall, can do no more than remark upon Walther's courage and upon how odd it all is.

When Walther embarks upon his Trial Song, he undeniably infringes a number of the rules of prosody set down in the *Tabulatur* (though for operatic convenience, he has of course only heard Kothner's shortened version): these are discussed in the chapter on Mastersong. He also upsets Beckmesser by apparently jumbling a number of *Töne* together, as well as by his lack of pauses, coloratura or melody. But Wagner is making a deeper, and sharper, musical point. Walther's complete song is indeed a *Bar*, but one cast in an original pattern, with the first two *Stollen* as A1–B1/A2–B2 and the *Abgesang* as C. When Beckmesser has heard what he takes to be a completed A–B–A, he angrily intervenes with his full slate of alleged errors, genuinely believing the song to be over at the point of its cadential return from an orchestral dominant seventh to the opening key of F. He is, perhaps, further irritated by Walther opening in F for his A1, crossing a more indeterminate tonality for his B1, and resuming on A2 with the same opening notes (to which Wagner now slyly gives the chord of the relative minor). Beckmesser's shortcomings, it should be remembered, concern his pedantry, not his ignorance: he has correctly heard an A–B–A form, as far as it goes, not appearing to realise that it is going further. The other Masters are merely confused. It is Sachs who comes forward to defend the song's originality, and to insist that it should be concluded. Walther does conclude, picking up on his B2 in the midst of a welter of argument, from which Pogner desists; but Sachs is the only one actually to listen, and to perceive the logic of the song (quite apart from his appreciation of its melody and expression) as a striking extension of *Bar* form.

Wagner is by no means finished with this point. So far, Walther has shown a natural disposition towards *Bar* form, then, under pressure in the Trial, an inventiveness with it whose irregularity confuses the Masters and irritates Beckmesser, but whose imaginative boldness seizes the mind of Sachs. But Sachs is also the one to realise that Walther needs guidance and discipline if he is to bring order into his invention, and achieve mastery. In Sachs's workshop, Walther is told to make his own rules and then follow them, so that by subjecting his imaginative vision, his dream, to the discipline of form, he may preserve it as art (the suggestion that each work of art requires its unique and unrepeatable form is of course good Romantic doctrine, one of many instances in the opera of Wagner himself speaking).

The ensuing Prize Song is a complicated structure. It falls into three parts, two dictated to Sachs, the third sung to Eva as Walther returns dressed for the Festival (and this is all planned with marvellous understanding so as to give the song a functional role in the drama between Walther, Sachs and Eva). With the first part, Sachs approves Walther's opening *Stollen*, also the second, observing that though it incorrectly ends in a different *Ton* (in fact, on the dominant, G, rather than the tonic, C), he is willing to learn from the innovation. The *Abgesang* which Walther is now told to compose picks up on the dominant and returns the music to the tonic – except that Walther's final C is harmonised with a seventh on a bass F sharp, the horn taking Walther's C to sound Sachs's *Wahn* motive. The second part is similarly A–A–B, ending this time on an augmented triad to reflect Sachs's emotion. The third part is the same A–A–B (though it ends on the former F sharp seventh chord, this time harshly scored as it drives Eva to collapse on Sachs's breast). The completed Prize Song is now thus not a true *Bar*, A–A–B, but A–A–A.

However, this is not its final version. As Cosima was the first to point out, the sentiments of Sachs's workshop were scarcely appropriate to the Festival, and their dramatic function was one that could not be repeated; and many others have drawn attention to Wagner's art in avoiding exact repetition of the Prize Song. Walther has only sung six bars when Kothner, charged with following the written music, lets the paper fall from his hands in his emotion; and Walther, noticing this, proceeds in a more free manner. This is not only free melodically: in the second stanza he allows himself to take the music through the boldly remote key of B major, which is of course the key of the midsummer magic. The entire song is now compressed into a single *Bar*. Wagner is making his final point about Walther's creativity. Having reconciled his natural skills to the Masters' rules, and learnt the benefits of their sense of order, Walther is able to create on the spur of the moment an inspired but disciplined Mastersong that wins their wholehearted professional understanding. His rejection of their offer of brotherhood in art is thus more than a piece of petulant rudeness; it is a failure to understand what he has achieved, well earning Sachs's reproof.

Walther's artistic progress is bound up with the course of the plot, dramatising the stages by which Sachs also succeeds in turning the *Wahn* of disarray to an artistically triumphant *Wahn*. But the philosophical striving for resolution underlying this is a constant condition of the opera, which takes its musical language from the tension between order and disorder, and the tensions within these, which were suggested earlier. The contact of opposites that is implied by tension can find fullest artistic expression in music, and particularly in harmony. *Die Meistersinger* is commonly held to be Wagner's most robustly diatonic mature opera, but this is to underrate the subtlety and the unique quality of his chromatic harmony in the work, and its place in the whole tonal concept.

C major is the key of the work's healthiest, most secure, most confident aspect: it is the key both of established civic order and of artistic achievement. The *diabolus in musica* opposing this is F sharp. It is the note which most acutely identifies the challenge to order (both creative and destructive), and Wagner's uses of it are among the most potent expressive devices of the opera. It is connected harmonically to C as part of the chord of the diminished seventh, F sharp–A–C–E flat, a chord which had long been a standard expression of horror in Romantic harmony, but which in *Die Meistersinger* has a subtler expressive force. Though not a motive, it is the chord of *Wahn*, containing both C and F sharp, two aspects of *Wahn*, and is itself an illusory chord in that it has no root, and can modulate in virtually any direction. Wagner, in the *Wahn* monologue, expresses the struggle within Sachs by drawing the F sharp down through a chain of thirds to C, as has been suggested; but the chord itself, and the relationship between C and F sharp, play a pervasive role in the opera. (This first occurs in passing, when David follows his lesson to Walther by advising him to give up his 'illusions of Mastery' – *Meisterwahn* – on the notes C–F sharp). Sachs's need to make this musical reconciliation, representing his determination to find human reconciliation, is adumbrated in his previous great monologue, when he sits under the *Flieder* reflecting on the song he has heard from Walther in the trial that morning.

The phrase that sets Sachs's mind turning was first sung by Walther to the words 'es schwillt und schwallt, es tönt der Wald' (spring, dispelling winter, 'swells and resounds, the forest rings'), repeated as spring is described as flooding the wintry woods with new sound, and taken up again matching the imagery with that of new blood throbbing in the singer's awoken heart. Ex. 7.1 shows Wagner's harmonisation of the phrase.

Example 7.1

The melodic beauty haunts Sachs; and Wagner's changing harmonisations have the force of drawing the utmost out of it as it is repeated, representing the resonances growing in Sachs's imagination. The phrase hovers in his mind, and drifts into it again under the elder. Here, he tries to banish all this confusing poetry by setting to work with his cobbling, but the phrase will not let the poet in him alone. He can feel it, he acknowledges, but not understand it, can neither grasp it nor forget it, for it had no rules yet no faults, it sounded so old yet so new: 'Es klang so alt, und war doch so neu'. It is only when he accepts that emotional and artistic necessity have justified it that he can at last sing the phrase himself – 'Lenzes Gebot, die süsse Not' – to the most impassioned orchestral statement yet (Ex. 7.2).

Example 7.2

The most intense chord here, recurring in the various statements and crowning Sachs's rapturous phrase, is the dominant minor ninth on D, which remains in different statements of the phrase though it may be approached and resolved differently. It can be no accident, in a score so beautifully devised, that the chord at this pitch is also a diminished seventh, F sharp–A–C–E flat, on a root of D; though the chord is in its third inversion, with the bass C helping to preserve tonal stability in the key of F as the dissonance is increased.

Here, the balance between opposing elements in the work is held in a moment of exquisite insight. Elsewhere, the F sharp will

frequently stand for disruption, but the threat of chaos is time and
again held in tension against the thrill of emotional adventure.
The Nightwatchman's horn sounds F sharp, first cutting across
Walther's furious, destructive tirade against the Masters who have
rejected him and threatening to force Eva to make the break from
Nuremberg with him. He conducts this in a long, tonally unstable
outburst (including some tritonal figures abusing the Masters) that
ends on his anguished top C as part of a harsh diminished seventh,
F sharp–A–C–E flat, from which the Nightwatchman picks the
F sharp; but immediately, as Eva soothingly takes his hand, the
F sharp becomes the dominant of B major, and the music of the
midsummer magic is sounded. The Nightwatchman's call ends
with his repeat of his F sharp, taken up by the apprehensive Sachs
with the words 'Üble Dinge' – 'wrongdoings'. The riot comes to a
climax on a dominant ninth on F sharp, with the Nightwatchman
again sounding F sharp as the midsummer madness is turned to
midsummer magic. The apotheosis of this magic is achieved in the
quintet, where conflicting emotions remain but are subsumed into
a lyrical outpouring in F sharp (notated as G flat), approached in
a chromatic descent from C and released in a modulatory process
leading to the C of the *Festwiese*. Here, and here only in the work,
the F sharp is no longer a note in a chord but generates its own
sustained key.

By such varied means, and by many more, the contrasts and
tensions of the 'F sharp' element of *Wahn* are composed. The tensions within the C major area are, naturally, of a different kind,
and accorded different treatment. Indeed, it is of the essence of the
splendid opening theme identified with the Masters that it should
not be capable of much modification, certainly not much harmonic
modification. It stands for civic grandeur, also for hard-won
values that can hold against threat, from within Germany or from
without (the lightening of it, in E flat, for the apprentices, in no
way mocks the theme, but rather confirms that it is supported by
a rising generation in its own mould). However, the grandeur is
dangerously close to pomposity, the assertion of values without
sufficient examination; and this lays it open to seeming empty at
various points when it is denied its sumptuous scoring and pro-
prietary C major. The bassoon version before Beckmesser takes the
stand as Marker is in a far from assured D minor; the apprentices
hand Kothner the *Tabulatur* to a heavily emphatic version (*schwer,
sehr markiert*) in A minor; the altercation between Sachs and

Beckmesser after Walther's song has an edgy version in C minor; and the bassoon statement ending Act I, after the Masters have left Sachs alone brooding in the church, is in F, showing them, at the close to this act in which their formal meeting to honour their art has taken place, in an uncertain light, driven from their original tonic to the subdominant. In Act II, as Walther angrily quotes Pogner's demand for Eva's bridegroom to be a Mastersinger, their theme is quoted with contemptuously light scoring, and its C major statement in the middle of his tirade in no way serves to assert their authority but rather shows them up as plain and limited in the context of his chromatic fury.

But C major is also the key of the chorale that opens the first scene, an unequivocal expression of faith and one uniquely German in its connection to the Reformation of which the historical Hans Sachs was an eloquent defender. This prepares, across almost the entire length of the opera, for the overwhelming emotional impact of the welcome to Sachs in the *Festwiese* with the opening of his own poem, 'Wach auf', hailing the new dawn of the Lutheran Reformation and now set by Wagner to another chorale. This is in G major, the dominant of C, onto which it resolves for the shouts of greeting – immediately touched with a bass F sharp as Sachs, moved by their affection but also disturbed by his sense of *Wahn* in a way they will never understand, can at first find no words with which to respond. And C major is, of course, throughout also the key of Walther's Prize Song, both in Sachs's workshop and eventually in the *Festwiese* – the good *Wahn* which Sachs has helped him to achieve. It is a musical consummation that this C major should have been brought into a union with F sharp (G flat) in the Quintet.

It is only in the context of such tonal relations that *Die Meistersinger* can indeed be held to be Wagner's most powerfully diatonic mature work. Though he moves easily and freely across keys, there is not consistently present, as a central musical characteristic, the intense chromaticism, constantly threatening to annihilate key sense, which marks *Tristan*, the work from which *Die Meistersinger* was intended as a relief. Yet it would be a mistake to regard Wagner's diatonicism as in any way straightforward. His use of third-related keys, declared already in the overture, was by now a standard feature of Romantic harmony (in his case perhaps consciously inherited, like much else, from his admired Beethoven, who in turn learnt it from Haydn). But his approach to chords, and their expected resolutions, is personal not only to him but to this opera. The brief examples quoted above of Walther's Trial Song give an indication in miniature of how standard chords can be used in original relationships so as to express particular words or phrases and their changing dramatic context. His fondness for augmented chords may have been one of his many acquisitions from Liszt. It is applied particularly to Beckmesser, for instance in the scene when Sachs hammers on his last to mark Beckmesser's faults in his serenade: Sachs's 'Jerum! Jerum!' introduces it, destabilising the harmony for the ensuing scene (and destabilising Eva, who realises that it is aimed at her and Walther as well as at Beckmesser). Augmented harmony consequently marks the riot as Beckmesser is beaten, and so survives to recur prominently in the scene when he stumbles into Sachs's workshop reliving that dreadful humiliation. Wagner's handling of the dominant seventh is at its most varied and individual in *Die Meistersinger*, since he is invoking the strengths and qualities of a diatonic normality while showing the hidebound that a novel approach can still be made to it. Frequently he will resolve a dominant seventh onto an unexpected degree of the scale, or onto another dominant seventh. He makes copious use of dominant ninths and elevenths, sometimes resolving them onto a dominant seventh. As Carl Dahlhaus has suggested, in connection with the 'Wach' auf' chorale, he can make use of dissonance while repressing chromaticism, delaying resolution of seventh chords by inserting intermediate chords and at the same time writing progressions suggesting pre-tonal music.[2] But these, and similar progressions, do not disturb the sense of tonality, as is characteristic of *Tristan*; they expand our experience of the possibilities of tonality.

'Es klang so alt, und war doch so neu.' None of the above techniques is unique to *Die Meistersinger*, but Wagner is applying them in a particular manner. His intention is to make us hear a diatonic style which is not a pastiche of some former musical age (and in any case, the canons of the musical language recreated have little to do with the sixteenth century), but which speaks to the mid-nineteenth-century mind in contemporary language of an order associated with older stabilities. Sachs's remark further indicates that there is no simple contrast between 'old' and 'new'; after all, a central theme of the opera is the bringing of the old, when it has become threatened by ossification, into the context of the new, and the disciplining of the new, if it is unclear and improperly formed, with the virtues of the old. There is a continual movement between the two, sometimes even as a simultaneous presentation; and this essential characteristic of the opera should act as a warning to any commentator who is tempted to try to contain the work's creative nature within too neat a theory. Indeed, because it takes a stand for the necessity of creative adventure and risk, it is bound to express this in music that is exploratory, essentially developmental and evolutionary.

The leitmotives are an articulation of this, the outward expression of the work's inner life. As such, they have a nature and action which are individual to it. In *The Ring*, which Wagner had interrupted in order to write *Tristan* and *Die Meistersinger*, an arpeggio, a rhythm, some juxtaposed chords, even a pair of notes, can act both referentially and symphonically; and in *Tristan* a single chord is made to have motivic significance. *Die Meistersinger* makes latent motivic use of a chord, the diminished seventh; but as an opera concerned with the creation of melody, it approaches its own creation of melody with a new fluency. It is possible to relate much in the melodic invention to the *vier gekrönte Töne* which Wagner found in Wagenseil. Plate 3.2 shows the typical opening of one: the shape characterising the opening Mastersingers theme (Ex. 7.3) appears in the last six notes of the first line (and in the *Abgesang*), and the shape associated with the banner of the guild (Ex. 7.4) appears in the first six notes.

In this *Ton*, also, is to be found the outline of the opening phrase of the Baptism chorale on which the curtain rises (Ex. 7.5), and its immediate near-inversion.

Example 7.3

Example 7.4

Example 7.5

It is not difficult to see relationships between this and a number of other significant themes or phrases in the work. That in David's song about the Baptist in Sachs's workshop is simple enough (Ex. 7.6).

Example 7.6

But the phrase of a falling fourth followed by a rising half-scale (or its inversion) permeates the invention more subtly, and with modified intervals and shapes. It is to be heard in the repeated phrase that so haunted Sachs's imagination (Ex. 7.1). This in turn lies behind the opening phrase of the Prize Song (Ex. 7.7).

Example 7.7

By now, moreover, the shape has also become associated with Eva (Ex. 7.8).

There are of course many more such instances throughout the length and breadth of the score. However, nothing could be more

Example 7.8

mistaken than to try to establish the original phrase from the
gekrönte Ton as an essential motive from which all follows, or as
some kind of motto or basic shape to which all is related. It is true
that a baptismal idea does run from it into various aspects of the
invention. But (even were the labelling of Wagner's motives ever
helpful except as a starting point for the listener's imagination)
this could not be labelled 'the Baptism motive'. For whereas in
The Ring and *Tristan*, motives tend to arise from, and remain in
some sense connected to, an original idea, in *Die Meistersinger* the
tendency is for motives to develop, sometimes with the association
of other material, into melodies with different applications.
Further, the evolutionary nature of the style means that motives
may also be embedded in a new and whole melody, whether they
generate it or form an incidental part of it not being the issue. The
outcome is that longer melodies than are usual in other of Wagner's
works characterise the opera, and also provide the opportunity for
complex relationships between them in certain scenes.

No scene in *Die Meistersinger* is emotionally more complex
than that in the workshop when Eva comes to see Sachs before
the Festival. Her excuse is that she is there to complain about her
shoe not fitting. Sachs is not taken in by this ploy: she has really
come to find Walther and – which is where her emotions are in
turmoil – to talk to Sachs, partly out of her old dependence on
his guidance, but also to try to maintain the amorous element she
has earlier declared in this dependence in case she is denied
Walther's love in the Festival and must choose a Master for
husband. It is only when she perceives the depths to which his
own emotions have been stirred that she stops dissembling and
addresses her great cry of love and understanding to him. Between
her and Sachs, her and Walther, and Sachs and Walther, love and
friendship are poised in a balance of extreme delicacy. In another
opera, Wagner might have approached this situation by use of
referential motives, perhaps attached to the characters or to a
previous expression of their emotions. He does not reject such
devices in the work (there is, among many other examples, the use

of the Nuremberg theme in the *Wahn* monologue), but they are not the means he uses here. Eva enters, to the broad orchestral theme of her conversation with Sachs in Act II; and this settles to the melodic fragment of Ex. 7.8, producing a tune shared between oboe and clarinet (Ex. 7.9).

Example 7.9

This continues to take new melodic forms, one evolving out of another, rather than the central figure being developed; but the figure permeates these melodies strongly enough for the outburst of the midsummer magic music now to seem to contain, in its third bar, a new melodic variant, generating a new conclusion (Ex. 7.10).

Example 7.10

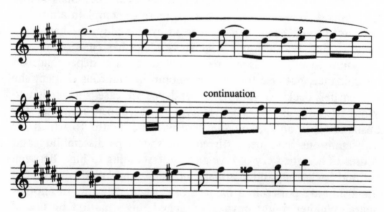

The Prize Song follows, it too now seeming a melodic evolution (Ex. 7.7). The song reduces Eva to tears, but it is upon Sachs's breast that she collapses, until he turns her away to Walther. His ensuing outburst against his cobbler's lot joins the phrase at the centre of the previous melodies to his cobbling song of Act II about Eve ('O Eva, Eva, schlimmes Weib') to make a new melodic conjunction. (Ex. 7.11).

Example 7.11

It is this, more than she can stand, which leads to Eva's outburst 'O Sachs! Mein Freund!', a tormented appeal to Sachs, to the feelings between them, out of realisation of what his renunciation means to him and out of her fear of what may yet befall her in the Festival (Ex. 7.12).

Example 7.12

So chromatically desperate is this, an outpouring of emotional complexity only previously suggested by the not wholly innocent Eva in her outbursts to Sachs and Walther in Act II, that it leads with ironic fluency to Sachs's rueful *Tristan* quotation. With the arrival of David and Magdalene, the baptismal origins of the phrase can be recalled (in chorale harmonisation) as the Prize Song is christened,

Ein-er   Weis - e   mild____ und hehr__   sollt__ es

hold_____   ge - ling-en

and then celebrated in the Quintet, in which the 'baptismal' figure and its inversion are at last united, and Eva's melody, evolving from her outburst, can also evolve into the Prize Song (Ex. 7.13).

Wagner has been much criticised for allowing a set number, the Quintet, into one of his mature operas, apparently against all his reasoning. Such comment is misguided. In the first place, the opera concerns the set number, the formal composition, as an artistic entity towards which men's art and craft must strive. But this would not hold were the Quintet not necessary to this scene both as a human and a musical summation. In human terms, Sachs has renewed his resolve to renounce any claim on Eva, in the presence of Walther, who probably does not fully understand the subtlety of the relationship between Sachs and Eva; if he feels compassion for the sorrowful cobbler, he does not do much to show it. Eva has made her peace with Sachs, however, and can turn to her true love. Walther has concluded his Prize Song with its final verse, and is ready to claim his bride with it. David has been promoted to journeyman, and can dream of marriage to Magdalene and the chance of becoming a Mastersinger himself; and these hopes are exactly matched by hers. It is the heart of comedy, the moment of comic truth, when all is poised for the happy resolution. And musically, Wagner with consummate craft and instinct draws together the complex strands he has been weaving in the preceding scenes, with his characters' tangled emotions, into a formal pattern. He could hardly have moved from the workshop directly into the Festival without a musical definition of what has taken place. His creative skill and his human instinct hold firm. Eva naturally sings the upper line, a lyrical outpouring but one of considerable metrical subtlety. Her melody lasts thirty-six bars, but these are divided irregularly into three sections, firstly four groups of three bars, then a thirteen-bar section that includes some four-bar phrases, then greater irregularity until she reaches her cadence with the others. Sachs, the next to enter, can confide to himself his continuing sadness; and though he knows he must not challenge her lyricism and must subdue his feelings in the interest of the greater good, he does find occasion for his emotions to flower in the phrase that opens the ensemble. Walther can share this phrase with David in thirds: perhaps it is a moment when the two men join their feelings of the promise of happiness. But however one interprets the lines of the Quintet, it is a necessary celebration, as they variously acknowledge, of the dream. This is the only significant word, *Morgentraum*, that they all sing, and it draws them into a circle of common experience. They are accepting, from intuition, instruction, experience, or study, what Sachs has taught Walther, that the artist's task is to preserve the vision that has come to him in the dream before wakening to reality, and to do so with the exercise of the greatest craft of which he is capable.

It is scarcely surprising that all the other important motives have a melodic nature: none is primarily associated with a harmonic progression or a rhythm, as is possible in *The Ring* with, for instance, the Tarnhelm or the Nibelungs. That of Walther's wooing occurs as the first lyrical theme in the overture (written, it will be remembered, before the opera) (Ex. 7.14).

Example 7.14

A figure of romantic yearning (Ex. 7.15) is also associated with him.

Example 7.15

His passion for Eva takes its first lyrical shape (Ex. 7.16).

Example 7.16

This moves easily into a version of the figure that is to find its most intense definition as the phrase that haunts Sachs's mind in Walther's Trial song (Ex. 7.1). The whole of this passage is an extraordinary adumbration of the melodic techniques that define the work; for not only is lyricism honoured, but phrases of the melodies can join or re-form, as they do later in the opera. The overture, it might be added, anticipates further ideas which characterise the opera, including dominant sevenths resolving unexpectedly, thirds-related keys (from the central tonality of C major), and fluent chromatic melodic counterpoint that can confuse the eye, though not the ear, as well as some near-Baroque counterpoint for the apprentices (perhaps still at their techniques exercises?). A further theme, arising from the apprentices, indicates the ability to mock the pretentious (Ex. 7.17).

Example 7.17

The famous combination of three themes (Exx. 7.3, 7.4 and 7.16) finds Wagner himself at risk from the Beckmesser in his listeners, though it is to the understanding of the Sachs in them that he can confidently appeal. That Sachs himself does not feature in the overture has been the subject of much comment. The only answer can be the simple one, that at the stage when Wagner wrote it, he had no idea of how Sachs would grow from the figure of his Prose Drafts into one of the greatest of all his characterisations.

Virtually none of the motives acts principally as simple identification of the person concerned, for such is not Wagner's way here. Two have a part to play in connection with Nuremberg itself, one with its grandeur and nobility (Ex. 7.18).

Example 7.18

Another is the riot that threatens to tear the city apart (Ex. 7.19).

Example 7.19

Of a similar nature is the theme associated with the Feast of St John, Johannistag (Ex. 7.20).

Example 7.20

David does have a particular theme (Ex. 7.21), but it is used principally to introduce him, and again to do so in Act III as he enters Sachs's workshop, and does not play much in the way of a developmental part in his character.

Example 7.21

There is no Magdalene motive, nor even a single Beckmesser motive, though he has a characteristic theme of malice (Ex. 7.22).

Example 7.22

This is perhaps best seen as bitterness and envy, distorting the qualities which Walther seems to possess, with false relations and emphasis on the tritone (Ex. 7.23).

Example 7.23

Sachs generates musical ideas that are warm, reflective and melancholy; but not even he really has a motive apart from the theme associated with *Wahn*, which is a perception unique to him (Ex. 7.24).

All the above material is melodic by nature, carrying with it problems for the composer. That is to say, though some of the themes are composed so as to be able to evolve into new melodic forms, each one of these (no less than those which remain more or less unaltered) has melodic individuality. The question therefore arises as to how the various melodies are to be made functional, as generating constantly evolving forms, but no less as themselves at any given moment in the drama; and the handling of this is one of Wagner's greatest compositional feats.

Example 7.24

Placed at important points are the songs which are sung in character on the stage. Such are Sachs's cobbling song, Walther's Trial Song and Prize Song, Beckmesser's serenade and attempted Prize Song, David's song to Sachs in his shop, the various Guild songs, and the two chorales, in church and at the Festival. Each is handled in an entirely different manner. Of the chorales, the first has a literal accompaniment from an off-stage organ for an actual congregation, while the second has a full orchestral accompaniment doubling the voices as if recreating the organ, but making more universal the imaginative potency of the Lutheran chorale: it is only with the cries acclaiming Sachs that the orchestra resumes its independent role. The Guild songs are simple melodies, descriptively enhanced but not commented upon dramatically by the orchestra in the continuous music of the procession into the Festival meadow. David's false start, as he remembers Beckmesser's tune by mistake, is unaccompanied; when he gets the melody right, its chorale-like nature is touched on by orchestral comments. Beckmesser sings twice. His attempt at the Prize Song, garbling the words but also producing near-nonsensical music, is at first accompanied only by his lute, and is later surrounded by puzzled and then unfriendly comments from chorus and orchestra alike; its clumsy nature isolates it from the rest of the music. It is similar in idiom, and in treatment, to his serenade in Act II, which is subjected first to Sachs's hammer blows and then, with the increased orchestral tumult, survives until he himself is subjected to the blows of the outraged David. Sachs's cobbling song is in a deliberately plain, hearty manner, ironically at odds with the harmony's depiction of the inner pain of the words. Walther's 'Am stillen Herd' is a special case, for though it is not sung, unlike his Trial and Prize Songs, it is a narration that has enough of the metrical condition of song to awaken the interest of the more perceptive Mastersingers. The Trial and Prize Songs, unlike Beckmesser's sterile songs to his sorry lute, are given an orchestral accompaniment to suggest the creative range of Walther's melody. Each of these (with the exception of the Guild songs) has in common a gesture 'presenting' it, separating it out from the normal course of the music, and tends to a metrical regularity that further separates it from the score's general melodic language.

Pogner's address to the Masters in Act I – a speech, not a song – is an example of something needing a different melodic approach. Especially by comparison with the conversational tone of the Masters' roll-call which has gone before, it has a strong, shapely melodic line introducing the St John's Day motive. Its first long section, describing the Feast, develops the narrative together with development of the melody, using flexible phrase lengths yet retaining a certain formality so as to dignify its utterance. A recitative section voices concerns about the decline of the burghers' reputation, before a return joining Masters and St John motives (it may also be noted that the recitative moves from the key of F onto an F sharp, going to C before returning to the tonic F). It is this kind of approach that characterises most of the extended solo addresses, including the impassioned outbursts by Walther and by Eva, though naturally each has its own distinct character. It marks Sachs's address to the people in the final scene before the Prize Song, and his final address (which balances Pogner's address in Act I, with its anxious central section, tonally disjunct and in a kind of recitative), and also marks the nearest the opera has to a sustained duet, the section in which Sachs instructs Walther in the nature of the poet's work in preserving the illusion of the dream in art. Here, too, there are passages of a more strongly melodic nature at crucial moments ('Mein Freund, in holder Jugendzeit'), with a more or less continuously evolving orchestral accompaniment.

So that an important part of the expressive burden can rest upon melody at these crucial moments in the opera, it is necessary for them to stand in contrast one to another, but also in some kind of relief to much in the conduct of the plot. Wagner's famous phrase *unendliche Melodie* never meant a perpetual melodic flow. It is remarkable how much of the score of *Die Meistersinger* consists of recitative, itself organised at different levels. The greatest virtuoso demonstration of this is David's lecture on the art of Mastersong to the perplexed Walther, which moves both wittily and touchingly in and out of a kind of *recitativo stromentato* to sudden eloquent curves to longer, more lyrical utterances. Of a different order is the succeeding scene as the Masters gather. Here, as often throughout the work, brief, recitative-like phrases carry on the conversational exchanges, serving to throw the expressive burden on the orchestra. It is perhaps an unexpected characteristic of the work that there should be so much recitative, sometimes plain though more often turning graceful phrases, sometimes given a token accompaniment though more often admitting expressive lines or developing a freely expanding, richly thematic orchestral texture. It is also often overlooked how slender the orchestral resources can be, how much of the opera is like chamber music, for a work whose tone seems to be set by the grandeur of the opening and confirmed by the ceremony of the close.

It should come as no surprise, though, to find that the character whose music ranges the widest across these melodic characteristics is Sachs himself. He has it in him to sing the tune of his cobbling song; but of course it is in the two great soliloquies that he is most fully revealed. The *Flieder* monologue begins, and continues for much of its length, in plain recitative phrases, with the expression contained in the tension between these tentative, searching phrases and the elusive melody in the orchestra which he cannot quite grasp. The contrast with his rough cobbling music as he thrusts all this aside is beautifully controlled, and his return to Walther's phrase, as it becomes more and more part of his imagination, finds his own melodic line moving from recitative into more lyrical phrases that are crowned with 'Lenzes Gebot, die süsse Not'; his gentle reflection on 'the bird that sang today', closing the soliloquy, consists of eight bars of pure, lyrical melody.

The *Wahn* monologue makes a different progression from the tentative to the confident, matching the harmonic framework. Sachs's bewildered dismay at the ever-present *Wahn* has him uttering disjointed recitative phrases, with the orchestra at first interjecting uncertain chords until the *Wahn* theme builds up, and with it Sachs's stronger melodic definition. Then his vision of a peaceful, untroubled Nuremberg, a pedal C anchoring the F tonality, brings with it a firm melodic outline that crumbles away with the tonal and rhythmic deterioration of the intruding riot. Yet the true recovery of C major from F sharp does not require his melodic contribution, which indeed could draw attention away from it, and he has only separated phrases; though there is great artistry in the placing of 'Johannisnacht' on a top E (the highest note in his vocal range) dropping an octave so as to make possible the confident scale from E up to the C in the new tonality that crowns the whole soliloquy with 'Johannistag!' Words (their shape, sound and order, and the ideas governing them) and music (harmony, melody, and orchestration) are composed into a whole that lies at the heart of the opera's achievement.

8 Stage history

PATRICK CARNEGY

The palpable sixteenth-century source material of *Die Meistersinger* has set it apart from Wagner's more myth-based operas, placing it in a backwater relatively untroubled by the attentions of 'producers' opera'. The fact that the work has, relatively speaking, not seemed a particularly promising case for interventionist stage interpretation gives a very special interest to the efforts of those bold enough to have attempted it.

Just how 'historical' did Wagner intend *Die Meistersinger* to be? For the purposes of the present chapter it is important only that Wagner, unlike his patron King Ludwig, had no interest in opera as 'dramatised history'. The subject matter and inspiration were, of course, Hans Sachs's Nuremberg, about which Wagner had read much. But Wagner's interest, like that of his contemporaries, was in creating a myth of old Nuremberg which corresponded to a present need that was certainly not for historical veracity. Sixteenth-century Nuremberg knew no fear of contagion from foreign arts. It had welcomed the Italian-inspired Renaissance and was at least as eager to cultivate relations with its close trading partner Venice as to celebrate its own artistic achievements. Mid-nineteenth-century Germany needed to believe in a Utopian Nuremberg that would represent a bulwark of national identity against political divisiveness and the pressures of modern industrialisation. Wagner, largely sharing this view, began by believing in the Nuremberg Mastersingers as material for a satyr play pendant to *Tannhäuser*, but ended by believing in them as a metaphor for his philosophy of art and the part it could play in German regeneration.

He knew the city from a number of visits, most importantly in 1861 when he arrived less than three weeks after the Deutsches Sängerfest. But when it came to the stage realisation of the opera,

135

he rejected the option of photographic exactitude in favour of whatever assisted the effective presentation of his drama. In the early days of Wagner's relationship with King Ludwig, the first performance of the opera had been planned for Munich. But in 1865 the composer and his patron were seized by the idea of christening *Die Meistersinger* in its name city. In Wagner's diary entries of 14–27 September 1865, written expressly for perusal by the King, the composer described Nuremberg as 'the home of the "art-work of the future"', and declared that the people must be shown 'clearly and unequivocally, in golden letters of fire, what is truly German, what the genuine German spirit is: the spirit of all that is genuine, true and unadulterated'.[1] The Nuremberg plan was later abandoned in favour of a Munich premiere as part of the celebrations for the King's projected marriage. Although the marriage never took place, the opera remained destined for Ludwig's Court Theatre. The premiere was set for 1868.

On Ludwig's initiative, and to Wagner's consternation, the court theatre painters Angelo II Quaglio and Heinrich Döll were despatched in June 1867 to do fieldwork in Nuremberg. When they reported back to Wagner (then living in Tribschen), he adjusted architectural literalness to serve the higher truths of art. The real St Catherine's Church of Act I (Wagner's original idea had been the towering Gothic edifice of St Sebaldus) was an undecorated 'monastic church with a flat wooden roof and the chancel ... covered by cross-vaulting'.[2] Working to Wagner's instructions, Quaglio (now assisted by his colleague Christian Jank in all the designs up to and including Sachs's workshop) created a composite fiction from the sketches he had made of several Nuremberg churches. This was a richly decorated interior with high windows more reminiscent of St Sebaldus's than of St Catherine's, and with emblems of Nuremberg's artistic prowess. Hans Sachs's famous house (17 Hans-Sachs-Gasse, formerly Spitalgasse, but destroyed in the Second World War) was plucked from the row it actually stood in and placed on a corner down-stage left (from the spectator's point of view) opposite the rather grander dwelling of the wealthy Pogner. Quaglio based Act II on Wagner's own marginal sketch, added by him in 1861 to the 1845 Prose Draft, showing Sachs's house on the left and on the right, across the street, the 'Haus des Ältesten'. Cosima Wagner's diary for 23 July 1877 suggests that Wagner may have had a particular location in mind, but this remains uncertain.

Wagner's demand that the houses should not just be painted façades but should be practicable solid constructions was a radical departure from usual German stage practice (though he would have been familiar with it from his knowledge of Parisian Grand Opera: he did not live to see the first Paris production, with sets by Amable, in this vein in 1897). 'The traditional flats', observed the *Neue Berliner Musikzeitung*, 'have disappeared in order to make room for the very embodiment of the town of Nuremberg with its houses, gables and projections. What one sees here are not painted houses but complete cardboard buildings, copied from real life, and streets, squares and perspectives so life-like as to deceive one into thinking them real.'[3] The *Festwiese* of Act III was Döll's Romantic interpretation of the Hallerwiese, the traditional site for festivals held outside the city walls.

Although the Court Theatre took the unusual step of using a guest stage manager, Reinhard Hallwachs from Stuttgart, to oversee the production, Wagner himself was actively involved. The opera's score is famously prescriptive of how its characters should move and behave. His remarkable mimetic gifts had, as the Vienna *Neue Freie Presse* reported, rarely been deployed to better effect: 'In a state of continuous excitement that makes one nervous, he accompanies every note sung with a corresponding gesture that the singers imitate as closely as they can; only someone who has seen the composer toiling and gesticulating in this way can have any idea of the multitude of nuances he wants to be conveyed ... One would regard it as miraculous if a production of the opera that was not rehearsed under the composer's supervision managed to introduce all the actions intended to accompany this music.'[4] The production team was augmented by a choreographer, Lucile Grahn, whose contributions to the staging included help with the street brawl at the end of Act II, and with the festivities in Act III. The premiere on 21 June 1868 was enthusiastically received. Hanslick, who had reason enough for antipathy (see p. 37), praised the opera as 'a theatrical experience' but deplored the music: 'Dazzling scenes of colour and splendour, ensembles full of life and character unfold before the spectator's eyes, hardly allowing him the leisure to weigh how much and how little of these effects is of musical origin.'[5]

Within a year of the premiere, the opera had been taken up by Dresden, Dessau, Karlsruhe and Mannheim, with Weimar, Hanover and Vienna hard on their heels, and the Berlin Court Opera House following in 1870. Despite Wagner's resistance, cuts were generally made, Vienna managing to prune the running time from about 4 hours 22 minutes back to 3 hours 30 minutes. The fact that Wagner had been allowed to watch the premiere, and to receive ovations from the King's box had, from the outset, lent authority to the work's status as an exemplar and symbol of German art. In whole, or in part, it met the need of the young German Empire born in 1871 for a work to dedicate new theatres or to celebrate patriotic occasions; and to this day it has remained *the* German commemorative festival opera.

Recognition of the opera's universal appeal was immediate, and by 1900 it had been given throughout Europe: Prague 1871, 1894 in Czech; Copenhagen 1872 in Danish; London 1882 in German, 1889 in Italian, 1897 in English; Amsterdam 1883 in German, 1900 in Dutch; Budapest 1883 in Hungarian; Brussels 1885 in French; Stockholm 1887 in Swedish; Milan 1889 in Italian; Madrid 1894 in Italian; Lyon 1896 in French; Paris 1897 in French; St Petersburg 1898 in German. It reached America with a Metropolitan, New York, production in 1886, in German. The basic scenery, modelled on that of the premiere, remained unchanged for decades; so that, for instance, Carlo Brioschi's *Festwiese* set for the Vienna Court Opera in 1870 repeated the Munich arrangement, with a wooden gallery for the Masters to the left under a spreading tree that arched over a distant view of Nuremberg. From the 1880s such 'improvements' as were made tended in the direction of increasing architectural verisimilitude. The Dresden production of 1869 may have been a notable exception. Hanfstaengel's photographs suggest a far more impressionistic treatment of the settings – like delicate watercolours rather than the saturated oils of the Munich realisation.[6] For the first Bayreuth staging in 1888, Max and Gotthold Brückner, working closely to Cosima's instructions, also copied the original but aligned the Act I setting more closely with the real St Catherine's by creating 'a plainly decorated, low-ceilinged and rather gloomy civic church' (see Plate 8.1).[7] Their Act II set shows Sachs's half-timbered house, a young *Flieder* growing by the door, and across the little square from which an alley leads, a nobler tree outside Pogner's grander house. Designers everywhere included ever more realistic Nuremberg details, incorporating, for instance, skyline views of the double spires of St Sebaldus and St Lorenz. It is worth recalling that general mid-century stage

Plate 8.1 Act I of *Die Meistersinger*, in the first Bayreuth production (1888).

practice saw little value in innovation. Theatres often did not invent their own scenery but bought it off the peg from design studios such as that of the Brückner brothers in Coburg, who, on the strength of having supplied the 'authorised' Bayreuth scenery (as they had also done for *The Ring* in 1876) could count on repeat orders from far and wide. Against Wagner's intentions, stage characterisations tended to emphasise Beckmesser as a caricature and stress the weightier, more philosophical aspects of Sachs.

Translating this atmosphere to other countries brought different interpretations rather than radical rethinking. For the La Scala production in 1898, which Toscanini conducted, the great Milanese set painter Carlo Ferrario transported (in Act II) a version of Dürer's house to a Nuremberg scarcely recognisable in the transformation of its architecture into Portuguese High Gothic: Sachs's little *Stube* became a capacious chamber filled with the tiled stoves, dressers, panelled ceilings, and hanging tapestries associated in the Latin mind with friendly Gothic clutter. But a portent of the opera's power in a sensitive political context was seen in Prague in 1898. Two acts given in the tenth anniversary celebrations of the New German Theatre provoked bitter exchanges between members of the city's Czech and German communities.

After a ten-year closure caused by the First World War, Bayreuth reopened in 1924 with a production which incorporated the minor modifications made in 1911 to the hallowed 1888 staging. Despite protests from a minority thirsty for change, its reassertion of conservative values accelerated the appropriation of the opera by a rising tide of national socialist sentiment. Erich von Ludendorff, one of the leaders of the Hitler putsch in the previous year, was present. 'Bayreuth's patrons', wrote Adolf Rapp in the programme, 'are gathered together in the camp in which everyone who wishes emphatically to be German increasingly finds himself'.[8] At the opening performance on 22 July the audience rose to its feet for Sachs's closing address, and at the end of the opera sang 'Deutschland über alles'. *The Times* (26 July) remarked that this was 'an extremely impressive demonstration, however little it may have been appropriate to the occasion, and however unseemly it may have appeared in the shrine where we are to hear *Parsifal* this evening'. Bayreuth ideologues like Hans von Wolzogen shrugged off the artistic context and enthused about the opera as a beacon of pan-German supremacy. By 1933, 'the names "Bayreuth" and "Wahnfried" no longer stood for the Festival and its artistic aims but for a limited ideology of Germanness which was national-conservative and antidemocratic'.[9]

The German emblem of the double eagle made its *Meistersinger* debut in the *Festwiese* for the 1927 Nuremberg/Fürth production, and avenues of German flags in the same scene had become commonplace by 1933. On 21 March of this year Wilhelm Furtwängler conducted a special command performance at the Berlin Staatsoper, in Hitler's presence, to commemorate the founding of the Third Reich. The work was elected official festival opera of the Party Congresses in Nuremberg, and here and elsewhere special attention was paid to the marshalling of the crowd scenes. However, restraint on some of the cruder audience reactions came from an unexpected quarter: the 1934 Bayreuth audiences found in their programmes a card reading, 'The Führer wishes to see an end to the singing of "Deutschland über alles" or the Horst Wessel Lied and similar demonstrations at the close of the performances. There is no finer expression of the German spirit than the immortal works of the Master himself. Gruppenführer Brückner, Adjutant to the Führer.'[10] For a new production which opened in Nuremberg on 10 September 1935, also conducted by Furtwängler, Hitler himself commissioned new sets and costumes from Benno von Arent, official set designer to the Reich, and personally vetted the preliminary sketches. Here the *Festwiese* was an undisguised celebration of *das Volk*, with characteristic party banners, from which only the swastikas were missing, looming high above the populace. *Die Meistersinger* bore the brunt of Nazi ideology throughout the Third Reich, and was the only work to be given at the 1943 and 1944 Bayreuth Festivals organised by *Kraft durch Freude*. In Bayreuth, orthodoxy reigned, as was emphasised in an article 'Bayreuths deutsche Sendung' by Friedrich W. Herzog in the Party newspaper, the *Völkischer Beobachter*: Herzog invoked Hitler's support, and claimed that there was no room at Bayreuth for 'the improvisation of repertory theatres' and that 'the recognition that in Bayreuth Wagner's works will be given "correctly", that is to say in the spirit of their creator, will always act as a magnet'.[11]

While there can be no denying that there is a powerful nationalist content in *Die Meistersinger*, this was an ingredient in a work of art and not a political programme. Wagner did hope that his art would help to engender a new political order in Germany, but it was not the Third Reich that he had in mind, and it is hard to imagine that he would have welcomed or condoned the use to

which the Nazis put his work. We know that he himself had
doubts about the more inflammatory lines of Sachs's 'Ehrt eure
deutschen Meister' address. At all events, their sentiments are a
mere fraction of the opera, and are not representative of the richly
complex human comedy as a whole. That this is so is abundantly
proved by the work's enduring popularity throughout the rest of
the world. In America, for example, performances continued
through both World Wars (though in England and France this
would plainly have been impossible). On the whole, the nationalist
element has not been an obstacle but has been understood as
integral to an artistic metaphor that is not a political prescription
for the real world. The Nazi-controlled press took a rather
different view, as when the *Frankfurter Zeitung* wrote on 7 August
1943, 'The German of our time can no longer wholly go along
with the resonantly Romantic primacy of art over politics
("Zerging' in Dunst das Heil'ge Röm'sche Reich").'[12]

 With few exceptions, *Die Meistersinger* has had little interaction
with ideologies other than that of the Third Reich. In 1928 the
Moscow Bolshoy Theatre wrestled with the choice of a Wagner
opera, finally settling on *Die Meistersinger* as 'far more ideologically
suitable than *Tristan*, which has the greatest display of Romanticism
and love in opera'. It was argued in favour of *Die Meistersinger*
that it has 'a wonderfully uplifting finale: bright, merry, joyful, very
suitable for our times'.[13] The Germanic elements were considered
no obstacle, Wagner's identification with the masses was asserted
and the story read as instructive of the class struggle. A contemporary lecturer described *Die Meistersinger* as depicting,

in addition to questions of art, the disintegration of a society which has
outlived itself over the course of historical development. The centre of
gravity in this musical comedy is . . . the satirical portrayal of adherents of
decrepit routine and the demonstration that the people are the only
competent judges of art and the source of collective artistic creation . . .
The main accent of the production should be placed on a well thought
out staging of the mass scenes and on bringing out the satirical elements
in the comedy.

 As for the role of Walther, the lecturer concluded that he is
'only the spokesman for free melodic creation, the sole source of
which is the popular masses'.[14] It seems, though, that theory did
not feed through into practice. The production turned out to be
very traditional, and was condemned as trite and cliché-ridden.
But it is significant for Soviet reception of *Die Meistersinger* that

as late as 1934 an important Russian book on the composer, after drawing attention to the proclamation of the opera 'by contemporary German fascists', could say that 'Hans Sachs is not only a symbol of Wagner, as a German artist of the period, but a symbol also of the whole national-liberal bourgeoisie, rejecting its revolutionary past for reconciliation'.[15]

In Germany itself in the later 1920s there had been an appreciable counter-current to the narrow-fronted national socialist adoption of the opera which remained in force at Bayreuth. At Frankfurt in 1927, Ludwig Sievert's designs set the emphasis for the production as a whole by placing, probably for the first time, Hans Sachs's house centre stage in Act II. For Heinz Tietjen's Berlin Staatsoper production of 1932, Otto Pankok produced Bauhaus-influenced designs. Sievert also designed a cleanly elegant production for Munich in 1943; and when he returned to the opera house after the war, at the Berlin Unter den Linden Theatre in 1955, he was able to elaborate his earlier designs without fear of being haunted by ghosts that he himself appears never to have invoked.

The laying of the ghosts of the Third Reich began almost immediately after the end of hostilities. On 10 May 1945, ten days after the end of the war, La Scala launched a new production with light, airy designs by Guido Marussig that showed scant concern for the evocation of historical Nuremberg. Plainly the production had been some time in the making. It was given in a temporary theatre, and the rebuilt La Scala (which had been destroyed in the war) opened in 1947 with the same production. Other theatres outside Germany soon had the work back in the repertory, though cuts were freely made, particularly of the more politically sensitive passages. German theatres whose traditional scenery had survived the war continued to use it. The images of a Utopian sixteenth-century Nuremberg and the message of the German spirit surviving must have been extraordinarily poignant and consoling in a country defeated and with so much of its heritage, including Nuremberg, lying in ruins. *Die Meistersinger* was again the natural choice for the reopening of rebuilt opera houses. The most significant changes made to the largely traditional scenery were in Act I, St Catherine's becoming a lighter, airier construction. Oswald Georg Bauer suggests that this may have reflected the widespread replacement of stained glass by plain glass in Germany's reconstructed churches.[16]

Bayreuth opened in 1951 with a conventional production by Rudolf Hartmann, but it was not long before Wieland Wagner came up with a radical treatment which dealt fearlessly with the lingering sense of unease about the misuse of which the work had proved itself capable (Wieland, as a twenty-six-year-old, had designed the sets and costumes for the 1943–4 production). If the heart of the opera was something other than a nationalistic anthem, then it ought to be possible to show this in performance. Wieland knew full well that the specific historical material of *Die Meistersinger* placed it apart from myth-based works like *The Ring*. The picture-cleaning task he set himself with *The Ring* was that of releasing the psychological and symbolic core from what had become a burden of unquestioned Romantic naturalism. In *Die Meistersinger* the task was not dissimilar, but plainly required a less abstract approach. To rescue the work from having become 'a dangerous mixture of Lortzing and the Reichsparteitag,'[17] the opera's images must be reborn. In Walter Panofsky's words, Wieland staged in 1956 'a mystery play about the secret of creative inspiration'.[18]

Act I revealed the congregation, posed as though in a devotional Renaissance painting, singing straight out to the audience, with the rudiments of a Gothic church (pews and carved wooden canopies), Eva and Walther in side-pews at the back, and sculpted images of Adam and Eve prominent above. The scandal of the production did not erupt until the midsummer madness of the second act. No trace of Nuremberg remained. The stage picture was simply that of a cobbled promontory, with a huge floral globe hung aloft and a smaller one on the right at stage level (see Plate 8.2). The simplest props – stool, work table, etc. – sufficed for the action. The air was suffused with violet-blue light. Wieland described the act as 'Richard Wagner's *Midsummer Night's Dream* – an enchanted, unreal world of elves and goblins', saying that 'a background of comfortable, old-fashioned houses would destroy its atmosphere'.[19] In Act III the *Festwiese*, with its view of old Nuremberg, had been handed back to a vision reminiscent of Greek theatre. In a steeply rising amphitheatre behind a small stretched-canvas stage in the foreground, the full chorus was already seated, facing out into the audience and seeming virtually part of it (see Plate 8.3). Instead of processions, the entries of the guilds were mimed by a single dancer. Characterisation played up the less agreeable side of the Masters' conservatism. The apprentices showed an earthy, medieval vulgarity far removed from *Lebkuchen*

Plate 8.2 Act II of *Die Meistersinger*, in Wieland Wagner's first
Bayreuth production (1956)

sentimentality. Despite the seductive impression of the photographic evidence, the Marxist critic Hans Mayer found the atmosphere in Act II 'lascivious and even bloodthirsty'.[20] Eva, Walther
and Sachs emerged relatively unscathed, though the latter was also
shown as a less than wholly honourable manipulator of the action.

The production created a furore, until then a most unusual
phenomenon at Bayreuth, but understandable in that this was the
first time that the picturesque scenery had been totally removed. It
was *Die Meistersinger* not only 'without the nineteenth century'
but also without sixteenth-century Nuremberg – and the degree of
abstraction, in which specific locales had been replaced by an
entirely different theatrical language (or strictly speaking, three

Plate 8.3 The acclamation of Sachs (Hans Hotter) in Act III of Wieland
Wagner's 1956 Bayreuth production

languages, one for each set: quotation, abstraction, narration),
could not help but be – and was plainly intended to be –
provocative. Many felt that the characterisations tugged too hard
against the music. In the repeat performances in the following
years Wieland compromised the abstraction of Act II (unsuccessfully, in my view) by adding a little fence round the cobbled
promontory, a token tree or two, and by sketching in the outlines
of a few gables and roofs in the background.

At the reopening of the Leipzig Opera in 1960, Joachim Herz
(with Rudolf Heinrich as designer) approached the work with a
critical realism born of his apprenticeship in the Realistisches
Musiktheater school of Walter Felsenstein's Komische Oper in
East Berlin. The basic elements of the set were two wooden
galleries, each of three tiers, ranged down either side of the stage.
In Act I they were used to suggest the nave of a church of late
medieval ambience, but here, as throughout, there was no attempt
at historical naturalism. The stage language was that of seeking

audience acquiescence in a 'let's pretend' style of theatre far removed from that of nineteenth-century illusion. In Act II the galleries became the backs of houses giving onto the River Pegnitz, which – making an uncanonical début in this act – was to be perceived, duly labelled in the Brechtian manner, as flowing down the centre of the stage. Much of the action took place on bridges thrown across the river to connect the walkways on either side. In their attempted flight by water, Walther and Eva hid under one of the bridges, where they were discovered and apprehended by Sachs.

For Act III, scene 1, Sachs's workshop was built as an inset construction. When it was struck for the *Festwiese*, the galleries were revealed as part of a sixteenth-century guild theatre, with a raised trestle-stage standing in the centre ready for the song contest. The guild processions were necessarily somewhat constrained, the various trades being mimed on the trestle stage as the populace gradually thronged the galleries to overflowing. Throughout the production, highly effective use was made of a forestage spreading out beyond the proscenium and drawing the audience closely into the action. Herz offered a markedly sympathetic portrayal of Beckmesser, who did not lack for supporters in the crowd. In keeping with the conciliatory mood of the production, Beckmesser did not flee after his humiliation but stayed on to hear Walther sing the Prize Song; Sachs offered him his hand, and Beckmesser brought himself to grasp it. Some degree of Beckmesser's rehabilitation, although counter to Wagner's advice to singers of the role, has often been followed since (in productions by Götz Friedrich, Stockholm 1977, and François Rochaix, Seattle 1989), no doubt at least partly to reconcile not only the rival Masters but also one of the darker strands in Wagner's ideology.

Wieland Wagner thought highly of Herz's production. Returning to the opera in 1963, Wieland restored it to the sixteenth century but now as a play, or series of plays, within a play, the framework being that of a Globe-style galleried wooden theatre (see Plate 8.4) in which a community caught in transition between what Hans Mayer described as 'the decline of feudalism and the emancipation of the bourgeoisie'[21] enacted the opera as a coarse comedy, as an entertainment staged by mechanicals. Wieland's argument was that Wagner's comedy 'had no need of the conventions of illusionistic opera-theatre'.[22] His approach therefore owed something to Brecht's theory of presenting a sequence of actions rather than representing them as 'real'. The curtain was replaced by a front-drop with the

Plate 8.4 Wieland Wagner's second Bayreuth production (1963): final scene.

title in Richard Wagner's hand and his signature. The church was signified by a triptych altarpiece (copied from a Lukas Cranach original), later obliterated by flying in a screen boldly inscribed with the *Tabulatur*. (Religion, of a kind, supplanted by art, of a kind.) Hans Mayer remarked upon the nice detail of some of the congregation kneeling in the old Catholic tradition while others stood 'in the new manner of the Reformation'.[23] The galleries and ground-plan of the wooden O, with the help of minimal props, lent themselves readily to the intrigues of Act II, though the unimaginative complained about the Nightwatchman's progress through the upper as well as the lower galleries. Act III began with a relatively conventional set-up for Sachs's *Stube*. Beckmesser's pantomime was not played literally but as though the *Stadtschreiber* – presented as a formidable intellectual on whom the Masters relied for a correct representation of the Nine Muses – was reliving the humiliation and pain of the previous night only in his mind. After a perfectly symmetrical positioning for the Quintet, the *Stube* was flown out, leaving the theatre ready for the rough and tumble of a Brueghel-like peasant dance which evolved into a conga, with the girls from

Fürth drawing the entire company into a single human chain. Fanfares from trumpeters on papier mâché horses heralded the arrival of the guilds with banners not of their trades but of the Nine Muses. The Masters crowded on, with Pogner borne in on a silver sedan chair. 'The whole impression', wrote Walter Panofsky, 'was that of an improvised farce like the play of Pyramus and Thisbe presented by Peter Quince to the court.'[24] Then the knockabout comedy stopped. After Sachs's address, a drop hid the wooden theatre from view and the chorus, now in earnest, sang their praise of Sachs straight out into the audience from the front of the stage.

Panofsky's summing up was that the production realised the composer's own early vision of something with the character of a satyr play. Hans Mayer described the portrayal of Hans Sachs as 'a man who is on his guard, endangered and at times also dangerous ... A man who needs all his power and strength in order to tolerate Stolzing as poet and companion.' From Stolzing, 'this Junker from Franconia', emanated 'the aura of a robber baron'.[25] Eva, in David Cairns's words, was not the *süsses Mädel* of traditional productions but 'a ruthless redhead, hell-bent on getting away from home with her buccaneering young adventurer,'[26] and with Magdalene as her youthful companion. Wieland Wagner told Geoffrey Skelton that the tradition had erred in presenting the Mastersingers as patricians.[27] He therefore had them enter in the working garb of their trades over which, like academics, they put on the gowns of the singers' fraternity. These were a stalwart aspirant-bourgeoisie embodying that immortal spirit of German art which would survive even military defeat. For Skelton, this textually accurate presentation of the Masters defused 'the taint of nationalism from Sachs's words [in his closing address], or rather what Sachs's words are usually taken to mean'. Sachs, he continues, 'is in fact propounding a thought of irreproachable liberalism, almost indeed of pacifism. It is not through its warriors that a nation shows its greatness, he says, but through its artists.'[28] The Brueghelised Nuremberg community was not idealised or even presented sympathetically.

No-one supposes that Walther's compulsory membership of the Mastersingers' guild will mean very much. The opera's presentation of the relationship between the values of tradition and innovation in art is far from perfectly resolved at the end, and there may be little any production can do to help. But to have secured such a focus in the opera's final affirmatory bars, and to have freed it of uncomfortably nationalist associations could not help but be a major achievement in the opera's stage life. Some of those offended by this second production now pined for the more spiritualised treatment of 1956. They and others felt less than totally comfortable with the idea that supreme values may be more at home in a rumbustious, earthy context than on some more elevated plane. For some, Wieland's rumbustious satyr play was an evasion of responsibility. Marcel Reich-Ranicki shrilly demanded the denazification of Sachs, arguing that it was time for a production set firmly in a Nuremberg of the 1860s.[29] This idea was taken up in various places, notably at the Deutsche Oper in Berlin in 1976, and by John Dew and Wilfried Sakowitz at Mönchen-Gladbach in 1980, where, at 'Ehrt eure deutschen Meister', there was lowered a portrait of Wagner in front of which everyone knelt. In 1980 in the same scene at Mainz, in Franz Bernhard Gottschalk's production with Uta Meid's designs, Sachs was welcomed into Parnassus by a tableau of nineteenth-century musical masters posed against the façade of Wahnfried.[30]

Productions endeavouring to soften the impact of history by framing Die Meistersinger in the time of its composition – with or without irony or deflationary humour – have not been frequent. The more usual strategy for neutralising nationalist sentiment in the work has been to opt for anti-historical, quasi-abstract settings as in the unadorned shoe-box setting used by Herbert Wernicke in his 1984 Hamburg production (also seen in Paris in 1989). Illustrative detail was supplanted by images of stark, alienatory directness. For the opening chorale, the men and women, in nondescript modern dress, were segregated on either side of the central aisle and sang straight out at the audience as in Wieland Wagner's 1956 production. In the second act the walls of the box seemed to sprout a thousand doors and windows overlooking a centre-stage Lindenbaum. The third act followed August Everding's 1979 Munich production in irreverently playing the Festwiese as a scene from an Oktoberfest (the annual Munich beer festival). The characters were presented dispassionately and with sharply observed detail: Beckmesser made his entrance in a shabby mac and Homburg hat, carrying a suitcase from which he extracted his Master's gown. At the end of the evening he was not allowed his curtain-call until everyone else had taken theirs. The point of this did not, of course, appear to have been to proclaim Beckmesser the hero of the hour, but rather to make a directorial 'J'accuse' of audience complicity in the Nuremberg citizens' hostility towards him.

One suspects that *Die Meistersinger* will continue to be problematic for German directors for the foreseeable future. But directors from other countries have also wished to defuse the opera's triumphalism and nationalist sentiment and seek out fresh perspectives. In an extreme example at the Théâtre du Châtelet in Paris in 1990, Claude Régy produced the opera as, to quote *The Times*, 'a dark, mysterious tragedy', insisting on 'the ritualistic, quasi-fascistic masculinity of the mastersingers', and turning the work 'into a vast hymn to the Judaeo-Christian dark ages, complete with crucifixion, rain and fire'. Roberto Plate's minimalist set contained 'the action within a giant cube, with everyone dressed in shades of Luftwaffe grey, apart from Sachs'.[31] Whatever its intentions, the production provoked catcalls, continual interruptions and a riot in the stalls to rival the Act II stage equivalent.

By and large, *Die Meistersinger* has shown an extraordinary resilience in absorbing – and sometimes in throwing off – the modern stage's interactions with it. The historical subject matter, Wagner's lovingly detailed treatment and the immense cumulative power of the score create a robust inviolability. This perhaps makes no more than the obvious point that performances stand or fall on their musical merits – as witness the unforgettably radiant quality of the 1968 London production at Sadler's Wells Theatre conducted by Reginald Goodall. Glen Byam Shaw and John Blatchley's production was notable principally for its self-effacing skill in accommodating so expansive an opera to a relatively small stage. The designs, by Motley, adapted well when the production played a major part in celebrating Sadler's Wells Opera's triumphant rebirth later in 1968 as the English National Opera at its new home in the very much larger London Coliseum. Elijah Moshinsky's 1984 staging in the same house used designs by Timothy O'Brien to move the period forward to the seventeenth century, evoking a distinctly Dutch atmosphere without fully explaining or justifying the transposition. Graham Vick was on surer ground in his 1993 Covent Garden production, finely conducted by Bernard Haitink. Richard Hudson's spare designs shrank 'Nuremberg' to portable models of its famous buildings, thus cunningly distancing historicist echoes from Vick's spotlight on the opera's timeless human comedy. This was played out, once again, in Brueghel-inspired costumes but, unlike in Wieland Wagner's 1963 production, *Das Volk* was now portrayed affectionately and without caricature, apart from some perhaps pardonable licence in the vertiginous eruption of the rioters through the scenery at the end of Act II. In his role-debut as Sachs, John Tomlinson gave a flesh-and-blood characterisation of exemplary concentration, bringing out a wealth of significant verbal detail and new life to the Act III exchanges with Walther, Eva and Beckmesser. The latter was cleverly played by Thomas Allen as a suitor with a palpable vocal claim to success in the contest, a man driven to folly not by incomprehension of Walther's gifts but by his immediate recognition of them. This production discovered as direct a route to the heart of the work as one could reasonably hope for in the 1990s.

Radical treatments of staging and characterisation have largely fed back into a relatively conservative *Werktreu* central stream. They have not permanently altered the perception of the opera in the same way that, say, Wieland Wagner's and Patrice Chéreau's productions of *The Ring* have done. The basic health and indomitable vigour of *Die Meistersinger* is plain in the way it has washed away the stain of its annexation by the Nazis. The opera comprehends, forgives and celebrates on a truly universal scale. Nevertheless, productions that deal only with the surface never go far enough. The performance history shows that there are problems at the heart of the work which are not to be ignored.

The 'Wahn' monologue

Text V	*Score*
Wahn und Wahn !	Wahn ! Wahn !
Allüberall Wahn !	Überall Wahn !
Wohin ich forschend blick',	Wohin ich forschend blick
in Stadt- und Welt-Chronik,	in Stadt- und Weltchronik,
den Grund mir aufzufinden,	den Grund mir aufzufinden,
warum gar bis auf's Blut	warum gar bis aufs Blut
die Leut' sich quälen und schinden	die Leut sich quälen und schinden
in unnütz toller Wuth !	in unnütz toller Wut ?
Hat keiner Lohn	Hat keiner Lohn
noch Dank davon:	noch Dank davon:
in Flucht geschlagen	in Flucht geschlagen
meint er zu jagen;	wähnt er zu jagen;
hört nicht sein eigen	hört nicht sein eigen
Schmerz-Gekreisch,	Schmerzgekreisch,
wenn er sich wühlt in's eig'ne	wenn er sich wühlt ins eigne
Fleisch,	Fleisch,
wähnt Lust sich zu erzeigen.	wähnt Lust sich zu erzeigen ! –
Wer giebt den Namen an ?	Wer gibt den Namen an ? –
's bleibt halt der alte Wahn	's ist halt der alte Wahn,
ohn' den nichts mag geschehen,	ohn' den nichts mag geschehen,
's mag gehen oder stehen:	's mag gehen oder stehen !
steht's wo im Lauf	Steht's wo im Lauf,
er schläft nur neue Kraft sich an;	er schläft nur neue Kraft sich an:
gleich wacht er auf	gleich wacht er auf, –
dann schaut wer ihn bemeistern	dann schaut, wer ihn bemeistern
kann ! –	kann ! . .
Wie friedsam treuer Sitten,	Wie friedsam treuer Sitten,
getrost in That und Werk,	getrost in Tat und Werk,
liegt nicht in Deutschland's Mitten	liegt nicht in Deutschlands Mitten
mein liebes Nüremberg !	mein liebes Nürenberg ! –
Doch eines Abends spath,	Doch eines Abends spat,
ein Unglück zu verhüten	ein Unglück zu verhüten
bei jugend-heissen Gemüthen,	bei jugendheissen Gemüten,
ein Mann weiss sich nicht Rath;	ein Mann weiss sich nicht Rat,

Mann, Weib, Gesell und Kind,
fällt sich an wie toll und blind !
Gott weiss, wie das geschah ?
Ein Kobold half wohl da ?
Der Flieder war's:
    Johannisnacht,
drob ist der Wahn so leicht
    erwacht
Ein Glühwurm fand sein
    Weibchen nicht;
der hat den Schaden angericht':
ängstlich suchend flog er dahin
durch manches müde
    Menschenhirn;
dem knistert's nun wie Funk' und
    Feuer,
die Welt steht dem in Brand;
das Herz erwacht dem Ungeheuer,
und weckt mit Pochen die Hand;
die ballt sich schnell zur Faust,
den Knüppel die gern umspannt;
mit Faust and Knüppel da zaus't,
wer gern als tapfer bekannt:
und will's der Wahn gesegnen,
nun muss es Prügel regnen,
mit Hieben, Stoss' und Dreschen
den Weltenbrand zu löschen ! –
Ein Koboldswahn ! –
Johannisnacht ! –
Nun aber kam Johannis-Tag : –
jetzt schau'n wir, wie Hans Sachs
    es macht,
dass er den Wahn fein lenken
    kann,
ein edler Werk zu thun;
denn lässt er uns nicht ruhn,
selbst hier in Nüremberg,
so sei's um solche Werk',
die selten vor gemeinen Dingen,
und nie ohn' ein'gen Wahn
    gelingen.

Mann, Weib, Gesell und Kind,
fällt sich da an wie toll und blind;
und will's der Wahn gesegnen,
nun muss es Prügel regnen,
mit Hieben, Stoss und Dreschen
den Wutesbrand zu löschen. –
Gott weiss, wie das geschah ? –
Ein Kobold half wohi da: –
ein Glühwurm fand sein Weibchen
    nicht,
der hat den Schaden angericht't. –
Der Flieder war's: –
Johannisnacht ! –
Nun aber kam Johannistag ! –
Jetzt schaun wir, wie Hans Sachs
    es macht
dass er den Wahn fein lenken
    kann,
ein edler Werk zu tun.
Denn lässt er uns nicht ruhn,
selbst hier in Nürenberg,
so sei's um solche Werk',
die selten vor gemeinen Dingen,
und nie ohn eingen Wahn
    gelingen.

Text V (in square brackets) and score

Wahn ! [and] *Wahn* !
Everywhere *Wahn* !
Wherever I search
in city and world chronicles,
to discover the reason
why, till they draw blood,
people harass and torment one another
in useless, foolish rage !
No-one has reward
or thanks for it.
Driven to flight
he [thinks] deludes himself that he is the hunter;
does not hear his own
cry of pain;
when he digs into his own flesh
he is deluded that he gives himself pleasure !
Who will give it a name ?
It's the old *Wahn*,
without which nothing can happen,
either to change or to preserve.
If it halts somewhere in its course,
it sleeps only to gain new strength:
it suddenly awakens,
and then, see who can master it !
How peaceful, with its sound customs,
contented in deed and work,
there lies in the middle of Germany
my beloved Nuremberg !
But late one evening,
to prevent a mishap
caused by youthful ardour,
a man does not know what to do;
a cobbler in his shop
plucks at the thread of *Wahn*;
how quickly in alleys and streets
it begins to rage !

Text V

Man, woman, journeyman and
  child
fall on each other as if mad and
  blind !
God knows how that came about ?
A goblin must have helped there ?
It was the elder-tree: Midsummer
  Eve,
up there the *Wahn* is so easily
  aroused.
A glow-worm failed to find its
  mate;
it set the trouble off:
seeking anxiously it flew
through many weary brains:
now it inflamed them like sparks
  and fire,
it set the world ablaze;
the heart awoke to the monster
and roused the hand with its
  beating;
this swiftly clenched into a fist,
which eagerly grasped a cudgel;
with fist and cudgel there was
  pummelled
anyone known to be bold;
and if the *Wahn* will bless it,
it must now rain blows,
with cuffs, punches and thrashings
to quench the raging world fire !
Goblin *Wahn* ! Midsummer Eve !
But now is come Midsummer's
  Day !
Now let's see how Hans Sachs can
  manage
to guide the *Wahn* subtly
to perform a nobler task;
for if it will not leave us in peace,
even here in Nuremberg,
then let it be for such a work
that seldom in commonplace
  matters,
and never without a touch of
  Wahn, is achieved.

Score

Man, woman, journeyman and
  child
fall on each other as if mad and
  blind
and if the *Wahn* will bless it,
it must now rain blows,
with cuffs, punches and thrashings
to quench the fire of rage.
God knows how that came about ?
A goblin must have helped there:
a glow-worm failed to find its
  mate;
it set the trouble off.
It was the elder-tree: Midsummer
  Eve!
But now is come Midsummer's
  Day !
Now let's see how Hans Sachs can
  manage
to guide the *Wahn* subtly
to perform a nobler task.
For if it will not leave us in peace,
even here in Nuremberg,
then let it be for such a work
that seldom in commonplace
  matters,
and never without a touch of
  Wahn, is achieved.

Sachs's final address

The first twenty-four lines of Sachs's final address, apparently achieved without very serious difficulty in the first draft of the libretto (Text IV), are in the second draft (Text V) almost identical to the published version. However, the latter part of the address (see Plate 1.1) evidently caused Wagner more problems than anything else in this draft. Out of all his deletions and substitutions, he achieved the version in the fair copy (Text V). The following is a transcription, then translation, of this (see Plate 1.2), for comparison with the printed libretto and version set in the score.

> Verliebt und Sangesvoll, wie ihr,
> kommen nicht oft uns Junker hier
> von ihren Burgen und Staufen
> nach Nürnberg her gelaufen:
> vor ihren Lieb' und Fang-Begier
> das Volk oft mussten schaaren wir;
> und findet sich das im Haufen,
> gewöhnt sich's leicht an's Raufen:
> Gewerke, Gilden und Zünfte
> hatten üble Zusammenkünfte
> (wie sich's auf gewissen Gassen
> noch neulich hat merken lassen!)
> In der Meister-Singer trauten Zunft
> kamen die Zünft' immer wieder zur Vernunft.
> Dicht und Fest,
> an ihr so leicht sich nicht rütteln lässt;
> aufgespart
> ist einen Enkeln, was sie bewahrt.
> Welkt manche Sitt' und manche Brauch,
> zerfällt in Schutt, vergeht in Rauch, –
> Lasst ab vom Kampf!
> nicht Donnerbüchs' noch Pulverdampf
> macht wieder dicht, was nun noch Hauch!
> Ehrt eure deutschen Meister:

> dann bannt ihr gute Geister !
> Und gebt ihr ihrem Wirken Gunst,
>   zerging' in Dunst
> das heil'ge röm'sche Reich;
>   uns bliebe gleich
> die heil'ge deutsche Kunst !

Young knights so filled with love and song as you do not often come to us here in Nuremberg from their castles and their revelry: in the face of their love of plunder we folk have often had to band together; and when crowded together, people fall easily to brawling: companies, guilds, societies have had wretched encounters (as we've seen lately in certain alleys !). In the Mastersingers' beloved guild, other guilds have always recovered their reason. Strong and secure, they are not so easily shaken; what is preserved is a lasting legacy. Many a custom, many a usage withers, falls into decay, vanishes in smoke. Away with strife ! Neither blunderbuss nor gunpowder can restore what is blown away. Honour your German masters: then you will conjure up good spirits. And if you favour their endeavours, then even if the Holy Roman Empire dissolves in mist, there shall remain holy German art !

The original Prize Song

The most striking of a number of changes which Wagner made to the text of *Die Meistersinger* between the fair copy (Text V) and the final libretto as he set it concerns the Prize Song. In its original form, as Walther first sings it to Sachs, it is given as follows.

> Fern
> meiner Jugend gold'nen Toren
> zog ich einst aus,
> in Betrachtung ganz verloren:
> väterlich Haus,
> kindliche Wiege,
> lebet wohl ! ich eil', ich fliege
> einer neuen Welt nun zu.
>
> Stern
> meiner einsam trauten Nächte,
> leuchte mir klar,
> dass mein Pfad zum Glück mich brächte,
> mütterlich wahr
> helle mein Auge,
> dass es treu zu finden tauge,
> was mein Herz erfüll' mit Ruh'.
>
> Abendlich
> sank die Sonne nieder:
> goldene Wogen
> auf den Bergen reihten sich;
> Türme und Bogen,
> Häuser, Strassen breiten sich:
> durch die Tore zog ich ein,
> dünkte mich
> ich erkenn' sie wieder:
> auch der alter Flieder
> lud mich ein sein Gast zu sein;
> auf die müden Lieder
> labendlich
> goss er Schlaf mir aus, –

gleich wie im Vaterhaus.
Ob ich die Nacht
dort wohl geträumt hab', ob gewacht?

Traum
meiner törig gold'nen Jugend
wurdest du wach
durch der Mutter zarte Tugend?
Winkt sie mir nach,
folg' ich und fliege
über Stadt und Länder heim zur Wiege,
wo mein' die Traute harrt.

Kaum
dass ich nah zu sein ihr glaube,
blendend und weiss
schwebt sie auf als zarte Taube,
pflückt dort ein Reis,
ob meinem Haupte
hält sie's kreisend, dass ich's raubte,
in holder Gegenwart.

Morgenlicht
dämmert da wieder:
scherzend und spielend
Täubchen immer ferner wich;
fliegend und zielend
zu den Türmen lockt' es mich;
flattert' über Häuser hin,
setzte sich
auf dem Haus, dem Flieder
gegenüber, nieder,
dass ich dort das Reis gewinn',
und den Preis der Lieder.
Morgenlich
hab' ich das geträumt:
nun sagt mir ungesäumt,
was wohl am Tag
der holde Traum bedeuten mag?

Tag,
den ich kaum gewagt zu träumen,
brachst du nun an
in der Freiheit lichten Räumen?
Ist es kein Wahn?
Sie, die ich liebe,
die das Herz mir schwellt mit süssem Triebe,
sie steht im Glanz vor mir?

Sag'
ist es nicht die weisse Taube

lieblich und treu
wie der Jugend holder Glaube ?
    Ihr ohne Reu'
    ganz mich zu geben,
ihn zu weihn all Glück, all Heil und Leben,
    wie, Mutter, dank' ich's dir ?
        Sonniglich
    will sie mir erglänzen:
    nächtliche Schleier
decken mehr die Augen nicht;
    heller und freier
sah' ich nie ein Angesicht.
Ob dem Haupt ihr schwebt ein Reis:
    ob sie das bricht
    von dem Zweig des Lenzen,
    huldvoll ohne Grenzen
mir die Stirn' um Sanges Preis
    hold damit zu kränzen ?
        Wonniglich
    schönste Lebenstraum !
Des Paradieses Baum
    reichst du dies Reis
wohl unversehrt ich blühen weiss !

Far from the golden doors of my youth I once went forth, lost in reflection: house of my fathers, cradle of my childhood, farewell ! I hasten, I fly now to a new world.

Star of my beloved solitary nights, lighten the way, that my path may lead me to bliss; motherly and true, lighten my eye, that it may be worthy of finding what fills my heart with peace.

In the evening the sun sank low: golden clouds banked on the mountains; towers and arches, houses and streets spread out: I passed through the gates, I thought I knew them again: the old lilac welcomed me as guest; from sad songs it gave me refreshing sleep, as in the house of my fathers. Was I waking or dreaming in the night ?

Dream of my foolish golden youth, did the mother's tender virtue awaken you ? If she beckons me, I follow and fly over city and country home to the cradle where my beloved awaits.

Scarcely do I think I am near her, when white and   dazzling she hovers above as a gentle dove, plucks a branch, circles over my head with it, for me to seize in her gracious presence.

Dawn breaks again: playing and tumbling the little dove drifted away; flying and guiding she drew me to the towers; she fluttered over the houses, and settled on the house, opposite the lilac, so that I might seize the branch and the prize of song. I dreamt it in the morning: tell me at once what in the light of day can the fair dream mean ?

Day that I scarce dared dream of, did you break in the shining realms of freedom ? Is it no illusion ? She whom I love, who fills my heart with sweet longings, does she stand in radiance before me ?

Say, is it not the white dove, tender and true as youth's fair hopes ? To give her to me wholly without regret, to dedicate fortune, blessedness, life, how, mother, can I thank you ?

Like the sun she will shine on me: night's veil, cover my eyes no more; never did I see a countenance more clear, more free; over her head there nods a sprig; has she broken it from the branch of Spring, immeasurably gracious, to crown my brow sweetly with the prize of song ? Blissfully, fairest dream of life, you tender me this immortal branch from the Tree of Paradise !

On 12 March 1862 Wagner wrote to Mathilde Wesendonk telling her that these verses had been written after the melody, of which he sent her the opening phrase (see Ex. 1.2, p. 32). However, by September 1866, when working on Act III, he had become dissatisfied with the melody, perhaps in part because it had by now suggested too much in the melodic lines of Walther's two earlier songs. Accordingly he devised a new melody, drawing it in part out of ideas that had been growing with the work. He also came to find the text unsatisfactory once he had brought the work to this point, by when the potential of the imagery of Eve beneath the Tree of Paradise had grown in his mind with the actual writing of the opera; for by the end of the year he had completely rewritten the poem, in the form we now know. This also involved him in devising a new *Verballhornung*, as the Germans call it, whereby Beckmesser garbles the original words. He sketched four lines of this on an envelope; made pencil sketches (with corrections) of the new version of the Prize Song as sung in Sachs's workshop; sketched the second and third verses of the *Festwiese* version (overwritten with very untidily scribbled interruptions from the people and Masters) and then made a fair copy, adding on the back the ten lines from Sachs's final speech beginning 'Hab' acht!' (dating this 28 January 1867); and, finally, made a fair copy of the 'workshop' version of the Prize Song with pencil insertions of Beckmesser's *Verballhornung* and, on the back, a pencil sketch of the addition to Sachs's speech. This all consists of five sheets, collectively entitled Text VII in *WWV*.